CROSSCUTS THROUGH HISTORY

Crosscuts
Through
HISTORY

by

Dagobert D. Runes

THE WISDOM LIBRARY

a division of
PHILOSOPHICAL LIBRARY
New York

Copyright, 1965, by Philosophical Library, Inc.
15 East 40 Street, New York 16, New York.

Type set at The Polyglot Press, New York.
Printed and bound in the United States of America.

Distributed to the Trade by
BOOK SALES, INC.
352 Park Avenue South
New York 10, N.Y.

This same work appears enlarged and illustrated under the title
DESPOTISM: A PICTORIAL HISTORY OF TYRANNY.

To the Reader

This book has no beginning and no end. Who can fathom the inception of greed for power and lust? And who can foretell its point of expiration?

This I know for certain: Men and women intoxicated by sheer willfulness and ambition for dominance have forever endeavored and often succeeded in abusing the common people, may their exalted station have been acquired by cunning, ruthlessness, or by a lamentably unfair tradition.

I have made a serious effort to present the reader with a cross-cut of the story of despotism. The pages of this book are almost a random offering; they could be multiplied a hundred times over with variations only in the detail and in geography.

The story of despotism is a woeful tale of man's inhumanity to man, but in the dock not mankind deserves to be judged, but rather the few, the usurpers and imposters, the treacherous nobles and kings of the realm, the avaricious foes of the citizenry who masquerade as the workers' defenders, while they aim at the scepter over the proletariat.

It is those few who plan war by yelping for peace and drive the masses into a frenzy with hate appeals against alleged enemies.

Be they proclaiming a defense of Church or Mosque, Crown or Tradition, Race or Rights, the lords mean to attack, with themselves safe in the palace, no matter what fancy legends their slogans or bunting carry.

The common man is prone to hate and these masterminds know it well. They set class against class, faith against faith, race against race, by use of virulent hate, the secret potion of tyranny.

This book has been written *cum ira et studio*—with anger and purpose—to bring before the serious reader the other side of history, the side of the people, who never were the beneficiaries of these power maneuvers, but rather their victims. No matter who won, the people always lost. The victories of the conquerors are only wreaths on the graves of the common man.

There is no fairness possible in dealing with the evil despots, past and present, except to warn the gullible and the unaware of these very monsters stalking the public arena. The power schemers of today speak with the voice of Circe and once they succeed in drawing the innocent to themselves, they turn them into beasts, roving growling beasts.

I fervently hope these pages will bring out the macabre undertones in the Sirensongs of dictatorship and make the still unbewitched tie themselves, like Ulysses, body and soul to the mast of their ship, sailing for freedom and democracy.

D. D. R.

TABLE OF CONTENTS

The True Face of History

The sophisticated Romans referred to history as *"res gestae,"* which means "things done." Historians and historiographers later attributed underlying purposes and alleged teleological meanings to these things done. The Mommsens, the Chamberlains, the Hegels and the Karl Marxes exasperatingly busied themselves with an almost religious zeal at interpreting the obvious as revelations of mysterious purposes.

Some of these historio-prophets as well as historio-profiteers would uncover Divine Providence in one or another historical event. Others would see the same events as significant patterns in the development of man from a lower form of civilization toward a higher one, such events demonstrating a slow but definite development of a particular Darwinian concept or religious absolute idea. Then again, some would refer to such incidents as merely economic phenomena determined directly or indirectly by the agrarian deficiencies of the peasantry.

That means, if a particular avaricious and cunning schemer of blue blood or of the military set directed his efforts on conquest in common greed for self-aggrandizement, those mealy-mouthed prophets with hindsight would probe for the motive for such conquestial misdeeds, not in the black heart of the usurper, but rather in the windy tents of pitiful shepherds, the shaggy lean-tos shared by peasants and cattle, or the foul-smelling caves inhabited by scroungy fishermen. All these, as far as military campaigns were concerned, contributed their share by carrying lance or ax or supplies, having neither the knowledge nor the stomach for the grandiose plots of the golden-helmeted war lord they served.

Never in history have economic measures justified a war, although such cause has often been pretended; every war in history has been economically disastrous for all serious participants in it. Never in history have religious reasons justified a war, although religious pretense has occurred again and again.

Avaricious military adventurers, such as Mohammed and the Califs after him, crusading buccaneers, gold-greedy pirates of land and sea, have often carried the long sword hidden under a religious banner. But no sooner did they spot the intended victim, than they dropped the standards of the ill-used Lord and stormed about their business of kill and plunder.

Genghis Khan and his wide banner on nine legs fell upon his neighboring lands under the guise of liberal nobility, just as Cortez, Pizarro and the others fell upon the Indians as latter-day apostles of the poor, ascetic Hebrew preacher Jesus.

It appears that in history once an act of conquest has succeeded, the misdeed assumes the attributes of legitimacy. Traditional history appears to be the *de facto* recognition of every evil deed that failed to be stopped or eliminated.

Military adventurers who flourish by the battle ax and the hangman's noose are honored by the title of Emperor, and those whose appetite is only limited by their capacity to wade in the blood and the sweat of the people are respectfully referred to as Queen of the Realm.

Men like Caesar, Alexander and the conquerors of Europe and Asia from Attila to Hitler, and including the elegant kings and queens of France and England, the admirals, generals and double-dealing diplomats, were no better than large-scale destroyers of the peace, breakers of the law and offenders against the sanctity of their neighbors' homes and lives. They had no reverence for the just or fair or for the soul of their fellow creatures. Nowhere does the name of God and justice appear more frequently than on the banner and the shield of the conqueror.

Those who warn of war invariably shout of peace and security, and never was a neighbor puny enough not to have frightened the giant at the border into aggression.

History is filled with just wars of aggression, but never has aggression truly been just; similarly no robbery can be a deed of self-defense.

It is time to show the true face of history—the history of the people and not that of their exploiters, the history of peaceable people who were vanquished—and to show in the true light the persons of reckless ambition and malevolence who made the world we live in a jungle of mutual destruction for the glory and vanity and ugly avarice of the very few, their henchmen and their sycophants. From days so far back that for a record of them we have to dig for documents deep in the sands and at the bottom of the seas, to the very hour we

2

live in, the evidence of evil can be heard and seen and it is no less horrible to behold today than it was in the past. Indeed, no outrage committed by the tyrants of old can outdo those perpetrated before our very eyes in this very generation. More people have been put to death—men, women and children—in the most grotesque manner by Hitler, Stalin and Mao during the lifetime of the reader of this book than have been slaughtered in all written history. Perhaps, if we clearly and solemnly look at the past, our vision of the present will be more concise.

The Lies of Yesterday

One often encounters the tendency to regard history as an aggregate of data duly established and recorded. Nothing could be further from the truth. Events of the past more frequently than not are obscured by historians rather than brought to light. We have to examine history, just as we do current happenings, for the purposes of the original source of information, and apply to it the same value judgments as we do news of the hour.

History is not more than events of the day punctuating the past. To begin with, history does not present itself; it is invariably offered on someone's platform. And such historic offerings are to be treated with great caution. The person reading a Russian history published in September of 1917 will read of the giant Kerensky who smashed the Czarist empire and at the same time warded off the vicious attacks of a conspiratory Bolshevik group.

The text of the Russian history published six months later relegates the same Kerensky to a clique of double-dealing supporters of Czarist capitalism, enemies of the people, whom the Bolsheviki under the leadership of Lenin and Trotsky had saved from Czarism.

Ten years later we were offered a third history of Russia; this time the saviors are no longer Lenin and Trotsky, but rather Lenin and Stalin, while Trotsky is placed with Kerensky as an antisocial, political monster. Two more decades go by, with page after page ripped out by accommodating historians, and in 1957 the big leaf is replaced. It was not Stalin after all who was second man to Lenin, but rather Khrushchev. This time it is Stalin who walks the plank into historic ignominy.

Naturally, whenever and wherever these large personages

are down- or upgraded, their satellites are deftly dealt with, following them into oblivion, infamy or sudden elevation. History does not record itself. It is chronicled by a bought pen and perjured vision. It is difficult indeed to gather truth from this historiographic corruption and then to extract from factual analysis a proper moral judgment.

If one raises the question whether a general, ethical regulative exists that could be objectively applied to historic events, I would say that ethics is not as complicated as some make it out to be.

Precluding sophistry, I would say we all know what the great freedoms of men are. Only a pointless quibbler or one with a nihilistic purpose would endeavor to deny the goodness of freedom and the blessings of peace; and that those who deprive men of freedom and peace are evil indeed. In this sense we must reexamine the builders of empires, the great conquerors, the sword-handed unifiers, the grand-scale colonizers, and the shining apple of imperialism right through the middle so as to seek out the worm of war, hate and suppression. The moral aspects of the past are no less important than those of our living days. In fact, in order to understand present affairs we need to uncover the hidden past.

To come face to face with the truth of today, we must bare the lies of yesterday.

The Romans, for instance, have been depicted as bearers of a great and noble civilization, establishing law and order in the then known world, having unified a hundred tribes and nations into one great Imperium Romanum. The truth is that the Romans destroyed every known and unknown cultural center in the Mediterranean Basin, and far beyond it. They burned Alexandria and Jerusalem, Athens, Carthage and Corinth, indeed every Greek and Semitic city. They spared only the theaters, in which, however, they scorned to stage plays and games as the Barbarians had done. Instead, they drove captives of all nations into the cellars like cattle, before sending them into the arena to fight against each other or against wild beasts, for the pleasure of the *plebs romana*. And in this Roman Empire the law was rigidly on the side of the patricians, the debauched hierarchy of self-intoxicated Caesars and an opportunistic Senate.

For those who admire the aesthetic aspects of the sundry arches of triumph in Rome, may we spread before them the

4

sordid panorama to which all these art pieces of architecture directly led—arenas where men, women and children of a hundred European and Asian nations were pressed into a sanguinary circus for what is called "the glory that was Rome," which in truth was shame and blasphemy.

If to corral a hundred nations and tribes means to unify them, then the Romans certainly deserve this tribute. They had a goodly number of chroniclers who set down history in the Roman manner, and these scribes established a precedent for later historians by referring to the Roman Empire as the world. They figured that what was not known to them was not worth knowing, although beyond their reach and beyond the shock of their catapults lived nation after nation whose culture equaled those that the Roman Legions reduced to ashes.

It was not the wind or the weather that razed the temples and the libraries, the academies and the theaters and the artistic homes of ten million people. From the Atlas Mountains to the Nile and from the Hibernian Peninsula to Mesopotamia, and from the Mount Sinai Peninsula to the marshes of Scotland—it was the Roman torch that burned out the traces of now forgotten peoples and vanished civilizations; it was the Roman sword that reduced the better hearts and the finer heads to serfs and slaves. The philosophers and poets of Greece, the scholars and prophets of Israel, the architects and scientists of Egypt, the craftsmen of Carthage—where are they? They perished, like Archimedes, at the point of a Roman sword or were stampeded into the great Mediterranean corral.

To study history without considering its ethical implication is like studying law without an understanding of right and wrong.

A crime is not less meaningful because it occurred generations ago, and evil is no less pronounced because distant nations or remote ancestors suffered its effect; tyranny shall not be pampered because it succeeded nor shall goodness and nobility be trifled with because they failed.

The Despots

This Greek word, meaning "ruthless power," is indicative of the issues involved. Somehow sycophantic chroniclers of the day and reactionary historians of modern times have succeeded in endowing this concept of brute force with the dignity of tradition, divine ordinance and subtle legalism. That means that if one clever major-domo or general of troops, or some bigwig's puppet, took dynasty in some people's territory, his offspring—legitimate or bastard—was entitled to inherit the perpetrated usurpation with the approval of the three hand-maidens given narcissistic aristocracy—hired jurisprudence, appeased churchdom and ready-made tradition.

The practice of one ambitious adventurer, with presence of mind and troops, of swinging himself into the saddle of dynasty and then holding on for dear crown and scepter not only for himself but equally for his brood, goes back without doubt to the early tribal life of man. In some countries, like Egypt, once established dynasties lasted for millennia, due to well-organized support by a crown-operated combine of priesthood, jurisprudence and social customs. The crowned head owned all the lands it could defend, and all the people within its borders. All men, women and children were slaves to the crown, and the status of the so-called "free men" consisted merely in the Pharaoh's loosening of his reins upon them for the better functioning of government. Any time his whim wished it, he could tighten the reins and the grand vizier, the head priest or the chief judge would be sent back to carrying water buckets. Nobody mattered but the man or woman Pharaoh, which significantly means "the big house." Outside the big house, from Pharaoh to Charlemagne, and from Genghis Khan to Stalin, there was only the great army of servants, most of them with fear in their eyes and subservience in their demeanor. Even those few granted by the master the privilege of walking around in fancy dress, bemedaled and beringed, were in fact servants forever subject to the ill grace of their patron; like festival horses they strutted about, bedecked for the parade—but one wrong move and a raised eyebrow from above, and they would be sent back to the drudgery of the plow horse, or a fate much worse. Until the eighteenth-century era of enlightenment, and excluding certain isolated segments of our historical past, the masses of the world have spent their lives in more or less rigorous servitude to dynastic arrogance.

Many are the ways and means by which such dynasties were established. Some were direct, like that savored by Roman generals who, upon the death of Caesar, would have themselves proclaimed emperor by their mercenary troops and

6

march into Rome. Others crawled upon the vacant throne beneath the purple cassock of a cardinal. Some were pronounced legitimate successors by bewigged jurists, because paternal philandering had somehow resulted in no progeny in the official spouse. And then there are those who wound up topmost in the incessant struggle for succession, prompted and maneuvered by intriguing court advisers, corrupt counselors and regents. Rules of succession, like the Salic Law, excluding the female species, Pragmatic Sanctions, employing noblemen's agreements (which of course were never kept), innumerable regulations and proscripts, tainted by the raising of false and real religious issues—all these beclouded the already devious ways of dynastic succession. One thing is certain: the voice of the people was never heard in the secret chambers of royal cabals, and never did the people have a hand in the imperialist machinations of Europe. In this sense most of the books of so-called history, with which our youth is burdened and the mature bored, are not books of the history of the people, their lives, their works, their plans and reforms, but rather worthless chronicles of the selfish deeds of dynastic schemers and their accomplices, their self-seeking manipulations for personal power and glory, appended by a melancholy enumeration of mutual assassination by poison, dagger, and ax, involving father against son, son against mother, brother against brother, and kin against kin. The wantonness of the crowned heads of Europe is outdone only by their brutal exploitations of a hapless people put under the yoke of these blue-blooded monsters, not by God and not by law, and not by traditional honor, but rather by a secularized greedy church, by treacherous jurists, and by foul customs masked as holy tradition. It is time to relegate these dynasties of ill repute out of the books of history into a chapter in criminology—the Bourbons and the Valois, the Merovingians and the Carolingians, the Stuarts and the Tudors.

These and the other thousands of palace-proud and mansioneers, with their fancy heralds, standards and buntings of nobility, whose claim to distinction rests not on wisdom and beauty, or faith, but rather on the battle ax and the hangman's noose,—some of the proudest of them, like Charlemagne, could neither read nor write and kept bordellos in the king's castle, as in the Pope's Vatican. They lived for their lusts and luxuries, and brought pomp to their parlors and pestilence to the peasantry and the towns. They had no thought except those given to satisfy desires, and no ideas except those of expansion. It is for that very reason that until the era of enlightenment the peasants and the other small people of Europe lived and died not better, and often worse, than the people that had existed thousands of years before them in the west of Asia, or around the Mediterranean Sea. And when the people began to rise and finally break the chains and smash the walls, it was not because of the crowns, but in spite of them.

The freedom of the people begins with the end of dynasticism, and it is time to remove the remaining, almost ludicrous vestiges of dynastic tradition, with their pretentious titles of Baron, Earl, Lord, Duke and Marquis, if for no other reason than for that of historic tidiness. The place for this theatrical humbug is not on the mantelpiece but on the trash heap. The farce of today's aristocracy is an ugly reminder of the days when the kings and their nobles grew rich and corpulent upon the sweat and the blood of the man of the street and the man behind the plow.

Peace at the Lance Point

The ancient Hebrew proverb states the issue—even the best man cannot live in peace if it so pleases his neighbor.

We have been accustomed during the last two generations to regard peace as the unmitigated goal of all liberal and progressive people. In fact, there can be found in all periods in history men, philosophers and statesmen alike, who would endorse war as a way of regenerating mankind. The Roman Tacitus, for instance, considered war the best taskmaster of nations, and the German Hegel warned his people against becoming effete through long-lasting peace.

On the other hand, many of those who speak of peace do so only to cover up their own warlike intentions. Swearing peace to neighboring nations, they induce their intended victim to drop his guard and discontinue or slacken his war preparations. They, meanwhile, secretly accelerate their own military activities.

The Romans were most vociferous about their "Pax Romana," but what they meant was not peace for the people of the Mediterranean, but rather peaceful submission to the Roman Fasces.

In the year before Hitler fell upon Poland and France his agents flooded the world with peace propaganda, and successfully so; when he launched his attack, socialist and gullible France and England were totally unprepared for war. Men like Stalin or Khrushchev never cease talking of peace to discourage others from arming. Indeed, to paraphrase an old Latin proverb, "If you expect war, make your neighbors prepare for peace."

Wars do not come about by the wish of the people. They occur because one or the other political adventurer in his desire for self-aggrandizement is eager for military conquest. Not always is this desire so openly professed as in the case of Alexander of Macedonia, or Frederick of Prussia who stated, "I find my country too small; I wish to extend its borders." And both men did.

In ancient days, mercenaries were easily recruited by promises of high compensation and unrestricted plunder and rapine. In modern days, when war almost invariably requires industrial support and general cooperation from the people, a bellicose imperialist must gain the support of the masses prior to his expeditions of conquest. A good job of propaganda is an essential preparation for warfare. From time immemorial the masters of war have found hate to be the one great unifier of the broad masses, and war's most reliable and persistent ally. People will readily go to war once they have been imbued with hate, and will eagerly follow the leader who allegedly protects them from the hated. Persons ordinarily perfectly moral, quiet and good-natured can be made to perpetrate unbelievable outrages upon their alleged enemies; it seems that the senses of pity and tolerance can be blotted out by that one emotion, hate. Once Hitler succeeded in uniting the German people in common hate against the Jew, seventy million of the most cultivated people of Europe would fall upon helpless children and women and destroy them as if they were vermin. They would discuss the choking alive of infants as indifferently as they would the poisoning of potato bugs. On our own continent, Castro managed to drive his people into such frenzy and hate against everything American, that Cubans, who only a few months ago were sharing games and pleasures with visiting Americans, would

9

gleefully watch public executions of alleged friends of America and demand with emotional hysteria that others be stood up against the wall and executed upon almost anybody's denunciatory remark.

The Chinese under Mao, who are dedicated to the destruction of the democracies, are given daily training at their miserable communes on how to defend the Chinese shores against American attackers. Mao and his henchmen know that the Americans are not wading upon their shores nor are the wooden picks and rifles of any value; but they are aware of one thing: the power of hate—these daily exercises in hate are what they want and what they need.

Aggression is committed by nations, but it originates and is initiated always in the brain of one dictator.

Aggression is carried by the fever of hate, and this fever finds its way into the hearts and the minds of the people, but it originates always in the blackness of dictatorial avarice.

In all the wars of all the kings of England and France and Germany and Russia, of Spain and Austria, and all the wars of the ancient Augusti and Pharaohs, the Mikados and Khans, the Califs and Hetmans,—in all these wars, the peoples of the world, ancient and modern, had no quarrel with their neighbor across the river or across the mountain range.

The quarrel was always started by one ruler, to enlarge his realm or enrich his treasury. All wars are wars of conquest. All wars were the King's wars and not the people's, but it was that common people who were made to carry the burden and suffer the wounds and the bullets, to undergo the tortures and experience the pangs of hunger and cold.

The people have no voice in the making of a war; they are the victims of war no matter which side they are on. Like the Hessian soldiers, when they won they went back to being serfs; when they lost, they were sold as serfs.

In modern days, the kings and the dictators make wars and then the people make the peace, until another dictator comes around and drives the people again to war.

The road to peace travels over the burial mound of dictatorship, and as long as we have dictatorship talk of peace will be no more than that. History has taught us that the more a dictator talks of peace, the closer he is to war.

10

Liege and Leech

One of the most useful concepts employed by suzerains to secure their unlawful positions and their hereditary transfer to the kinfolk is loyalty. In its Latin meaning it implies legality. The concept of loyalty rarely appears in history without the appendix of an oath, which lends it a certain religious and legal connotation. Once loyalty is sworn, its breach would be an affront to the heavens as well as to judicial etiquette. So deeply was the mind of the commoner confounded as well as exalted by the magic of the holy oath, and the law of the realm, that in the main he would live on his knees in loyalty rather than stand up and tear apart the cobwebs of religious vows and king-serving laws.

Loyalty to the liege, obedience before the law, and submission to the will of God—these three matters made up a powerful chain with which to keep a world of people in subjection.

But in truth loyalty was not legality if arrogated to himself by a dictator; law serves no justice if it is the mistress of the tyrant, and religion is not binding if it becomes the handmaiden of a usurper.

If a peasant or townsman becomes liege to any lord, he is not loyal, but only subservient, because the overlord himself has broken the fundamental rule of God and man, that no one may hoist himself upon the body of his fellow citizens and make himself a master over his fellow creatures. No oath of allegiance given to such overlords is valid if extracted under deceit, at the sword-point, by supplication, or through superstition. All the deeds of these avaricious and ambitious princes, ill-conceived and misbegotten, deserve their place in the records of crime and not of history.

Majesty belongs solely to the Divine Principle, whence the great prophets of all nations have drawn their strength to call for brotherhood among men; loyalty is due the God of love, and not some filthy queen or king dressed up in *Firlefanz* of plush and ermine and gem-studded crowns, staring down upon their genuflecting fellow men with theatrical grace and happiness.

It doesn't matter if they are as vicious as Catherine II, who reduced peasants and laborers, miners and soldiers, to a mass of evil-smelling serfdom, herself deeply engaged in playwriting and harlotry, or mere bores like Queen Victoria, seeking solace from widowhood with a boorish horse attendant, or a Hindu fakir, leaving the government to courtiers and diplomats.

In our days new kinds of lieges have come over the horizon, pressing for extreme loyalty among their subject comrades. These new overlords, flaunting hammer and sickle instead of crown and scepter, are no less overbearing than their princely predecessors. They, too, surround themselves with a guild of whispering flatterers, and punish slips of fealty, or even the suspicion of it, with as gruesome a coldness as the perfumed kings of Spain and France.

Of course their liegemen swear loyalty not on the Bible, but on the Communist Manifesto and in obedience to the laws of the People's Republics, but there is as little socialism in their subservience as there was Christian equality in those of the earlier ages. As far as the laws of the People's Republic are concerned, they are interpreted by ever-ready stooges and sycophants at the whim of the dictator, the Stalin and the Mao Tse-tung.

Russia under Stalin was a nation where fifty million people were doomed to labor camps, deprived of all comforts of life, bereft of kith and kin, dispossessed of all traces of freedom, and eking out a dull existence in misery, filth, coldness and overwork. In Stalin's Russia the people outside the labor camps had neither choice of work nor choice of residence, no right of speech or free assembly, no right to protest or disagree, no right of repudiation or appeal. All elective positions had deteriorated into personal appointments by the Lord Secretary himself. Citizens disappeared with a cry in the night, never to be seen again, while others were presented to the public in theatrical court procedures, terrorized, by torture and threat, into blabbering fantastic confessions, as in the days of the unholy Inquisition.

The pagan and the Christian Kings, the Czars and the Pharaohs, the Shoguns and the Shahs—they tied loyalty to them with the ribbon of God and the law. The dictators of the Fascist and Communist brand—the Hitlers and Mussolinis, the Stalins and the Mao Tse-tungs—they knotted loyalty to the Leader together with party principles and the welfare of mankind.

The Roman Caesars and the Catholic kings of Spain killed

the Jews because they refused to pray at their altars. Hitler and Stalin killed the Jews because they would not swear allegiance to those colossi of conceit.

To understand the Baal of today you have to study the Baal of yesterday. How far away is Octavianus Augustus from Joseph Stalin? How far away is Ferdinand of Spain from Hitler? And still they are the same.

They beat their brothers to the ground and set their foot upon their neck and put them to servitude like cattle. There will come a time when all symbols of oppression will roll into the sand—crown and scepter and hammer and sickle as well.

Chivalry and Brigandry

Much romanticized "chivalry" draws its origin from the Latin *caballus*, meaning "horse," and with good reason, because it is meant to indicate a superior kind of behavior and conduct, such as becomes a man on a horse. Already the ancient Romans had singled out the horse owners (*equites*) and the *patricians* (those whose fathers were legal) from the mere people, also known as proletarians who have nothing but offspring. The patricians were legitimate, they were legal —indeed they *were* the law, and the *equites* (those who could afford to ride instead of walking) were their equals. The plebs, on the other hand, lived only by the grace of the patricians and the *equites*. They held little power under the Roman Republic, and none under the Caesars, who kept them amused and docile by supplying them with *panem et circenses* (bread and circuses), while, lower yet on the rungs of the ladder of existence, in the Roman structure of society, hovered the fluctuating masses of slaves and bonded captives.

In the medieval society of Europe, where the princes and princelings flattered themselves by Caesarian imitation, we are again faced with this abomination of dividing living humanity into cavaliers, or horsemen, and the common people, mostly serfs with some few artisans and townsmen living a tributary existence at the greased-palm grace of the seigneur or sovereign.

In this Age of Chivalry, with its romantical deeds of reputed charm and generosity by errant knights, troubadours, benign men of the cloth, and God-fearing Crusaders, we find in

13

reality a bleak and bitter world of luxurious palace life up on the fortified hill, and rags, serfdom, disease and starvation in the valleys about.

I will say, however, that while the castles had their luxuries, their trumpets, fanfare, gilded portals and velveted women, there was always murder lurking in the niches, stairways and secret trappings. There was fratricide and matricide and patricide, and general sinister dungeonings and torture, inflicted upon friend as well as foe, upon the nearest of kin as well as upon the itinerant stranger or the invited guest. The cavaliers and their liege ruled by poison and dagger, as they judged by the rack and succeeded to each other's properties by treachery and the garrot.

With all that, they liked to brighten their evenings with songs and tales, not only with mead and wine and oriental spices. The ballad singers and troubadours were peregrinating varlets of spiritual sort, catering to those high at the table and their fanciful ladies.

And whose praise would they sing, these balladeers? Certainly not that of the serf behind the plow, or the townsman at the workbench, or the scribe in the sheriff's office. They would sing the glory of the man on the horse, the man on the throne, the man who paid the piper and would call him back again. El Cid—the sheik of Valencia, the Sire of the Moors—played Moslem against Christian, and Christian against Moor. It was he who served brother king to kill brother king, and hired himself out to a prince to rob his sister princess, a man who was no more than a battle ax on a horse, and a hired one at that, who changed allegiance at the toss of a coin. Yet through the pen of these purveyors of romance such men as El Cid assumed stature of sublime *grandezza* and infinite Christian virtue.

Through the pen of such literati, and through the wine-inspired tongues of sycophantic minnesingers, Rolands and their mythological figures of King Charlemagne and his ilk grew into starry-eyed, celestial barons fearlessly dedicated to bringing Christ to the heathens; while, indeed, known to all but the indifferent and the deceived, Charlemagne sent an army of mercenaries paid by the blood and the sweat of his serfs into Spain to cut himself a piece of the Moorish wealth and women—the first for other campaigns against his neighbors, and the latter for his harem in Aachen. His massacre

14

of the Saxons, women and children, or of the citizenry of
Lombard, his slave-hunting enterprises in the provinces of
the East—what horrible music would the true sounds make
could they be brought to us today, these horror cries of
mutilated humanity, victims of a power-greedy tyrant! But in
spite of the cries of those unfortunates, the ears of our young
and gullible are filled with sirenic melodies, false and de-
liberate, serving a twofold purpose: to cover the gruesome
truth and to lull our minds with romantic lies.

The chivalry of the medieval ages was no more than arrogant horsemen riding roughshod over the poor of the land,
the land of the innocent neighbor as well as that of the
native sons. If these cavaliers went abroad with their artful
weapons, hammered out of the poll taxes they took from the
meager earnings of the serfs and laborers, they didn't go to
serve the cause of goodness or justice or peace, but rather the
irrepressible wish of their liege or their own for loot of land or
loot of gold.

Take one of these crusading travelers, the much-romanti-
cized Richard I, lovingly referred to as "the Lion-Heart."
Perhaps panther would have been his more appropriate name,
as that creature is known to turn against its own. When this
gentle prince was only sixteen years old (1172), he joined his
two older brothers in an attempt to destroy his father, King
Henry II. In 1189, in collusion with Philip of France, he
succeeded in driving his father off the throne. In 1190 he
joined Philip II of France on a crusading venture to rob the
Orientals. Taking the city of Acre, he fell out with his cross-
bearing ally over the amount of loot to be allotted to each of
the two. Philip II preferred to return home. Another disagreement broke out with Duke Leopold VI of Austria, who ar-
rested Richard on his return from Palestine and released him
only after payment of heavy ransom, probably to make up for
the difference they had at Acre. The Lion-Heart had to pay
another ransom to Emperor Heinrich VI, who also held him
in arrest until delivery of the money. When Richard returned
to England he found his brother John had conspired with
Philip to dethrone him.

That is the stuff of which Crusaders were made. Perhaps, as
a side remark, I should mention that among the victims of
Richard's painful adventures, ending in the payment of huge
sums of ransom, were not only the serfs and townsmen of

England, but also the Jews in his territory. In order to rob them of whatever property they possessed, he incited a massacre in London and he, as well as his brother John, caused the suicide of the Jews in York Castle.

It may be that some of the epics and legendary tales involving the era of chivalry rate fair or even high as pieces of literature. But is the tune worthy of such a high price? Must truth and sheer humaneness be sacrificed as the price for these false, adulterated songs of romanticized glorification of kingly scoundrels and robber cavaliers?

Roman Peace

Rarely has a term and its public application been as much abused as the word "peace." Etymologically it signifies agreement; commonly it implies the cessation of hostilities, the absence of aggression. Roman peace, or *Pax Romana,* as it was officially proclaimed by the dictator Octavianus at the beginning of our calendar era, expressed well the state of affairs within the far-flung borders of the Roman Empire. There were no more active hostilities, there was little aggression—it had all been stamped out by the huge and swift mercenary legions. But soon enough that very same Octavianus would send his legions into Teutonic territory and elsewhere, not, of course, as acts of aggression but rather to preserve the Roman Peace. And for centuries to follow, the dictators of the Roman Empire continued to engage in defensive aggression and protective hostilities until they had spread their tyrannical rule over neighboring countries beyond the Black Sea, beyond the Euphrates River, into the deserts of Arabia, the far end of the Iberian Peninsula, and beyond the Atlas Mountains, in all cases making the neighboring lands subject countries or tributaries, exploiting them to the very bottom of their resources and selling into servitude huge segments of the native population, whether Gauls, Celts, Germans or Slavs.

Even when the Emperor Caligula conferred Roman citizenship upon millions of the free men within the Empire, this act was purely a clever scheme to increase the number of taxpayers because, at the time of the dictators, Roman citizenship implied no political privileges of any kind or participation in the government. Incidentally, this monstrous Caligula, one

16

of the successors to Octavianus, was the particular Protector of the Peace who expressed the wish that the whole Roman populace had but one single neck for him to break.

While the so-called republican past of Rome was blotted by many acts of imperialistic and bloody expansionism, including the sacking of Carthage, Athens, Corinth and a thousand other cities around the unfortunate Mediterranean Basin, the following centuries of Caesarian Rome were bloodier still.

The republican era wound up in the first century before our calendar in the struggle between General Gaius Marius, the Consul presented by the people's party (*populares*) and General Lucius Sulla, the leader of the conservative state party (*optimates*). The cruelties perpetrated by the victorious legions of Sulla upon members of the people's party were typically Roman in character. Thousands were mutilated and crucified. With Marius and Sulla we enter the era in Rome when the real power no longer rested with anyone but the commander of the legions. The old-time short-service citizen armies had disappeared, and the generals ruled the nation. Following Marius's death and Sulla's withdrawal, a triumvirate developed with three generals in joint command—Gnaeus Pompeius, the man responsible for nailing to the cross a whole army of rebellious slaves under Spartacus; General Marcus Licinius Crassus, like Pompeius an enemy of the people's party; and finally Gaius Julius Caesar, who managed to send Crassus to command a legion against the faraway Parthians in Persia, where he was assassinated. Now swiftly Caesar turned against the allegedly threatening people of Gaul. His successful and most cruel military campaigns were accompanied by a gory massacre in which men, women, and children were killed, and prisoners of war had their hands cut off. But they gave him an opportunity to obtain the increase of his military forces that he required for the destruction of Pompeius and to conduct two campaigns in Britain.

It is amazing that for two thousand years school-children of the Western world have been subjected to the compulsory reading, in the original Latin, of this megalomaniac's war memoirs.

After the devastation of Gaul and parts of Britain, Caesar marched against Rome in defiance of the powerless Senate, in a drive to exterminate Pompeius and his troops. In Egypt he finally put an end to his living rival. After that he devoted

17

his time to routing out and destroying all opposition to his one-man tyranny, partly by public trials, but mainly in secret and by the profligate use of paid assassins. In a very few years there was no one to be found in Gaul or Italy, Spain, Greece or Egypt, or anywhere in Asia, Africa or Britain, who would dare oppose the whip of the great Caesar. While Octavianus, his nephew and successor, set forth with great fanfare a proclamation of the *Pax Romana*, it was really Caesar who had established it. There was peace all over the Empire, the peace of a cemetery. But Caesar's glory was short-lived. On the Ides of March, 44 B.C., he was assassinated by a small group of Senators who had not yet been bribed or blackmailed by the general.

Caesar had previously designated as his successor his nephew Gaius Octavianus. The people of the European world were so awed by the name of Julius Caesar that those following him on the throne of tyranny adopted it as a cognomen of divine distinction. Until this very day his name is used by princelings who wish to emphasize their right to succession by Caesar's formula, "My blood will succeed me." This farce of succession by blood, in later centuries considerably strengthened by the pretense of divine ordination of the procedure, dominated the political life of Western Europe. Celestial predestination of royal succession by blood was strongly supported by the clerical, landed and titled gentry of Christendom, and they managed in their own little realm to secure succession of their holdings by the egotistical testament of the bloody old Roman general. He considered Rome his personal property, with all its 3,000 legionnaires and all its citizens, and he left it to his sister's kin, as one would deed a house or a boat or a chest of coins. Quoting as a precedent this whim of an avaricious dictator, equally selfish and corrupt men of power managed to establish, in many countries throughout the Western world, rules of succession that exist to this very day. These rules assume that the lands and the air, the waters and the plants, the people and what they create, are the mere subjects and property of some decadent princeling, just because his aunt or cousin or father or grandmother or uncle had usurped such Crown prerogatives.

In this sense Caesar left his mark on the Western world as no man had done before him. Many rulers aped the name, calling themselves Kaiser, or Czar, or Shah.

In spite of Caesar's testament, his nephew Octavianus found the going rough and had to settle for a temporary triumvirate, with Marcus Antonius, a distant relative of Caesar, and Marcus Aemilius Lepidus, whom he quickly eliminated. After involved political and military maneuvers, Octavianus managed to have Antony trapped with Cleopatra and won a decisive naval victory over them in 30 B.C. at Actium. Upon the subsequent suicide of Antony and the Egyptian queen, Octavianus became, as his uncle was before him, absolute master of the Empire. His fights for the supreme power, his political manipulation of a weak Senate and prominent patricians for his own personal advantage, became typical of the ugly struggles for the succession that beset the European scene for the next two thousand years. It is the detailed account of these struggles that is commonly known as history. To secure his possession, Octavianus issued a slew of reform edicts. He bludgeoned the Senate into giving him the right of censorship over its members, thereby reducing the Senate to a group of disciplined advisers, rather than legislators. He was responsible for the erection of many new temples, not only in Rome and Italy, but even in the colonies, and made it obligatory to offer temple sacrifices in his honor. Indeed, this demand that Caesar should be treated like a god was one of the most powerful causes of the Hebrew revolt. While Augustus increased the number of temples—in fact, he made Rome a city of marble—it is doubtful if he increased faith or fealty. We find that the Senate, which by now had about as much integrity or authority as the Reichstag under Hitler or the Soviets under Stalin, honored Octavianus by making him, in quick succession, first *Imperator*, which means commander-in-chief or Emperor, and then *Princeps*, which means something like Mussolini's *"Duce,"* Hitler's *"Führer"* or Stalin's "Leader of the People." A few years later Octavianus had himself elevated to the office of *Pontifex Maximus*, or High Priest, a title later cherished by the Popes and by some Emperors. In Britain Henry VIII, in proclaiming himself head of the Church, made the title ridiculous and his successors robbed it of all meaning. Octavianus also caused the month Sextilis to be renamed Augustus. This name was the first honorific title bestowed upon him by the Senate. To keep a check on the Proconsuls chosen by the Senate as rulers, for one-year terms, of the various far-flung provinces, he established personal ambassadors responsible to him alone. These exercised the real but hidden authority in the provinces, a system similarly developed in our time by Stalin and Hitler, who had secret agents or commissars paralleling the official administrators. Octavianus was a great road and fortifications builder, and established army bases throughout the Empire. He particularly encouraged the technical development of the armed forces. The patricians of Rome managed to amass great fortunes through the long regime of Octavianus, during which opposition in the provinces was driven underground and trade and commerce flourished. The main beneficiaries of the great wealth extracted from the colonies, with the help of the Proconsuls, were the patricians of Rome on whom Octavianus leaned heavily for advice and support. We find here again the phenomenon of tyranny and concentrated opulence sponsoring literature and the arts. It is the age of Maecenas, the patron of Virgil, Ovid, Horace and others. This awkward parallelism carries over for generations. We find it amazingly active under Claudius Nero (37-68); the last Emperor to be a member of the Caesarian family by blood, rather than by adoption. One of Nero's chief advisers was the Stoic Seneca, who penned moralistic essays on the virtues of poverty and asceticism, but who, as the personal treasurer of Nero, managed to amass fifty million sesterces. He was definitely involved in some of the assassinations engineered by Nero, and finally conspired against his master, who ordered him to commit suicide. In A.D. 59 Nero murdered his mother, and in 62 his wife. He had already murdered Britannicus, whose guardian he was. In 64 Rome burned, and Nero inaugurated the great Christian persecutions, accusing the Christians of having been incendiaries. However, having criminals, captives and slaves devoured by animals for the amusement of the people was a common practice among the Roman elite, and it neither began nor ended with Nero. Near almost every major military establishment of the Romans one can find these arenas dedicated to gladiatorial games and to contests between wild beasts and unarmed men, women and children. Even the philosophical Caesar, Marcus Aurelius, who, like Seneca, wrote observations on good morals, did not eliminate this practice. A cynical historian has observed that these circuses finally fell into disuse because Roman North Africa, whence Rome imported its beasts, finally ran out of wild animals.

Nero, like Catherine II in modern times, was somewhat of a poet and musician. and he espoused culture and literature. Perhaps the most monstrous of the ill-humored dictators of the Roman Empire, he was undoubtedly the most cultured of the lot, and in the intervals between unspeakable deeds of oppression and assassination he seriously favored the arts.

Out of funds extorted from the provinces and from Italy, Nero erected a magnificent palace, Domus Aurea (the golden house), and had burned-out Rome rebuilt with wide avenues and streets. However, the *Pax Romana* had come to an end and revolts broke out at the far ends of the Empire. Nero died by the dagger as he had lived by it. His generals systematically and successfully crushed all uprisings and, in the year of Nero's death, his successor intensified the campaign against Palestine which ended in the year 70 with the burning of the holy city and the diaspora of the Jewish people.

God and Gaol

The history of law is the history of man's injustice to man. In its meaning law implies set rules of conduct either traditional, religious or contemporary. As all rules of conduct have been determined, interpreted and enforced by the rulers of the realm, justice has always mirrored, not the goddess upholding the scales, but rather the man or woman behind the scales.

In early Athens the law was written for the eupatrids, the well-born or nobles, by such men as the seventh century (B.C.) Draco, who prescribed the death penalty for even the theft of a cabbage head. When some citizens pointed out that this was rather harsh retaliation, Draco replied, "This was the most proper fine I could think of for this little crime. I am sorry to have no greater punishment for the other offenses." The Draconic law provided the death penalty for barbarians and other strangers who were idling; natives who refused to work for the upper classes at the customary pittance suffered disenfranchisement.

It may be noted here, that in modern England, almost up to the time of the American and French Revolutions, the penalty for theft of any property in excess of ten dollars was hanging. Even children of twelve were executed in England (and, incidentally, some of the other European countries) for such offenses. Many volumes have been written by distinguished British barristers and solicitors, by philosophers and historians, on themata of law, but hardly a word—not even in Blackstone—about these horrible crimes perpetrated on the poor by the lawmakers and the law interpreters.

The great Decemviri of Rome, taking a page out of Draco, also interpreted the law for the patricians (the well-bred) and the equestrians (those who could afford to ride horseback). It stands to reason that the people of Rome had as little a case against a patrician as the people of Athens against the eupatrids.

As far as the serf of Central Europe and Russia, or the villein of England was concerned, for nearly two thousand years they had no remedy at all under the feudal and manorial system of law, because their respective lord was master, not only of their employment and faith, but also of their personal conduct; he was judge supreme. The sovereign could mete out justice as it suited him; he could castigate or deface, incarcerate or strangle, put to the torch or to the ax any man, woman or child as it suited his whim.

Much of the punitive cruelty, such as penal servitude, penal colonization, exile to penal isolation like Devil's Island or the ice-covered tundras of Siberia, so common even in contemporary European countries, is part and parcel of the feudal approach toward the offender, whose crimes were conditioned almost exclusively by his economic plight. The French as well as the Spanish, the Portuguese and, of course, the British, operated slave ships up to the nineteenth century, and, until then, the lash and the plank pointing out to the sea were the law for both prisoners in transit, and the impressed sailors as well. In our own twentieth century the lash was the law on the road to Siberian exile, and on the *via misericordia* to Germany's concentration camps.

Up to the recent centuries of at least partial enlightenment, the common people of the Western Hemisphere lived primarily as servants of their overlords, except for a comparatively small number of semi-independent cities of the post-Renaissance which managed to buy protection for their townsmen. The law, therefore, was interested, in the name of the kings and their kindred, only in the protection of their

22

property and the maintenance of subservience. In feudal times men who opposed the ruler, such as Henry VIII, would have their genitals cut out and burned in front of their eyes; others would have their intestines pulled out by executioners until they died in agony. Nothing that depraved human minds can think of in terms of bestiality, cruelty and savagery was omitted by the men who desired to force abject servility from their subjects, and trembling respect for their property and God-ordained position. It is this fanatical regard for the master's property that pervaded law to such an extent as to support killing a child for stealing a coat, and confining a chained man in a dungeon for thirty years for running off with a loaf of bread. I am not speaking of days of antiquity, but rather of times when clever essayists crowded the literary markets of London, and imaginative playwrights presented shows on the royal stage of Versailles; when Catherine II corresponded with other liberal minds, and the halls of Vienna, Madrid and Berlin were hung with tapestry and oils; when the ladies wrote fancy poems and played the harpsichord. During all this time of cultural enjoyment the voice of compassion for those who fell victims to the evils of traditional law was small and still. In all the centuries past, the deep legal, philosophical and theological minds spread their searching profundity into intricate, detailed crevices of the unknown, but very little understanding and feeling is there to be found for the man whimpering on the rack, or the woman shrieking under the bite of the white-hot tongs tearing at her breast.

These were not isolated cases, these were not singular criminals I am speaking of, but tens of thousands—nay, hundreds of thousands—of persons subjected to the poisonous fangs of the law, religious and criminal—for civil it never was.

These philosophers and theologians exuded chapter after chapter in manner mystic, scholastic and even geometric, on divine and moral laws. The word "love," falling often from their cold fingers and stony hearts, was as meaningless, as emotionless, as if it came from the bitter tongue of an Inquisitor.

What good is all that philosophizing and theologizing, if the very people who write about God as if He were a personal acquaintance, and of His love as if they were imbued with it, condoned or ignored all the judicial evil of their time in its gruesome, blood-spattered actions?

For all the laws they inscribed and described, they failed to see the injustice of their attitudes and actions.

Of all the crimes of the past, Law is by far the greatest. Law was little but a set of rules by which the rulers might keep the common people in bondage and obedience. The nations lived in gigantic prisons, and the laws were but the prison rules of the era.

Since then the wave of freedom has swept aside much of the unfairness that separated the common man from his God-given right to property, dignity and independence—at least in one-half of the world. But the law of old is still with us—much of it is.

If we look at the law of today, even in our own country, we find it much at odds with justice and heavily burdened with feudal tradition. In the state of Virginia a man of an alleged White Council—perhaps "Yellow" would be a better name for it—could stand up and with impunity address peaceful citizens, exhorting them to commit violence on their neighbors of a different color; when in a small group of his fellows, he would bedeck himself with symbols of violent Fascism. And even if this group were openly to advocate and even practice abuse of that minority, their punishment would hardly exceed a few weeks of confinement. On the other hand, in the same state an obviously impoverished person was given a sentence of seven years' incarceration for stealing a bag of chicken feed.

In another state the Governor declared his readiness to close all public schools if the Federal government were to enforce a system that would permit children of darker hue to sit with those of Caucasian color. This crime against the very Constitution of the nation was ignored by law and court, and their feeble attempts at interference were easily side-tracked; yet in the same state a widow with three children was sentenced to a lengthy prison term for adding to her meager state relief by accepting payment for small chores.

In hundreds of our cities, towns and villages men offend the dignity of a distinct minority of their fellow citizens by calculated humiliation in the form of placards, announcements and other signs indicating their undesirability. Such flagrant offenses against the law of man and the law of God are condoned or ignored, sometimes even encouraged, by the law-makers and law interpreters of these states and communities; those who commit them are protected in an obstinate and

24

cruel manner by police officers and sheriffs alike. And may it be said again, the church is silent, but this silence speaks no less emphatically than the justification based on established customs and traditions. It is easy to detect the illegality of the past; it is difficult to understand the illegality of the present.

It seems the eyes of the law can overlook almost any misdeed and misdemeanor—the maltreatment of minorities, the degradation of the weak, the oppression of the aged, ill and poor, the encouragement of gambling and alcoholism, the corruption of youth by display of the underworld in print and film. The law can overlook a thousand crimes of exploitation, if concocted with care by schemers and scoundrels, but the law has a sharp eye for any offense against property.

The law dwells on property offenses. It is a throwback to feudal days—or perhaps it never entirely emerged from them. All crimes are understandable except those against Crown property. You can beat a Negro boy to death for whistling at a white girl, and the law will look the other way, but let the man steal a bag of corn and he is in for it. You can kill four black people, as they did in Macon, Georgia, in 1946, and the law never saw it; but steal a car in Georgia and you will be on the chain gang for more years than the week has days. Drive a black girl out of a school with blows and four-letter words, and the law will see no evil; but run off with a ten-dollar bill from the counter, and the law will get you. In the good old days of the Wild West you could beat a man one-eyed, and the town would laugh; but steal a horse, and they would hang you.

The law puts no value on man's dignity, and little on his security, but an awful lot on his property.

In Soviet Russia you may abuse or insult the minorities, but if you change a donated ten-dollar bill through channels other than the State Bank they will shoot you. If you steal a pair of boots from your factory they will shoot you; if you steal a pig from the public farm they will shoot you. But if you call the Jews spies and exhort your neighbors to denounce them, the law doesn't see it. The law has eyes only for property.

The kings are gone, the nobles are gone, but their law is still with us. It is time to break the law of the past, and let us have the law of tomorrow—not with regard to property and position, but with regard to dignity and liberty, and the true independence of all citizens, and let those who fall under the pressure of economic strains be dealt with in a helpful manner toward rehabilitation, instead of being reduced to caged animals. Herding offenders into a corral and silent drudgery will make them into perverts sneering out of the sides of their mouths; it will make them neither better nor saner. Perhaps some day we shall have cities of rehabilitation where offenders against property and propriety will be taught a better life, instead of being jailed in a deeper tomb.

Cry for Freedom

One of the basic segments of man's essential being is the wish for freedom. This yearning can become so powerful that under certain circumstances it will run contrary to the obvious advantages of material existence. It can even make men lay down their lives to obtain a cherished victory for others, a victory beyond their own reach. The history of the ancient Greeks, Israelites and Carthaginians bears inspiring witness to such noble altruism, as do events in our own generation, ruthlessly subjected to multi-colored standards of oppression. Man's cry for freedom has never ceased to reverberate, but in the millennia of known history it has often been drowned out by the shouts of impertinent usurpers, their henchmen, viziers and subservient plebs.

In the Dark Ages of European and Asian history we sometimes have to search for the small voices of the freedom-loving; and, to be sure, even those were muted before their time.

In days of the Stone Age when most men lived as some bush tribes still do in Brazil or Australia, the overgrown head-hunter was master of the club wielders. In later eras the swordsman excelled; later still came periods in which the blue-bloods on the throne were sheltered against the winds of freedom by the persuasive interpreters of church and temple, subject only to mutual assassination by their own clan. The battles within and between the clans were not fought for the sake of freedom, but in the ripening of greed and controversy. Many and varied were the standards of tyrannical accomplishment, and a new chapter to this melancholy thesis has been written by a woeful history since the days of Machiavelli.

For those who assume, encouraged perhaps by hopeful school texts, that our century completely differs from the past on the score of freedom, may I say that outside the Anglo-American world (and the few nations of Western Europe that live under the tutelage of this group) there is no more freedom to be found today than in other times of the past.

Almost half of the world is strictly ruled by a small clique of so-called labor leaders who have labored as little with their hands as their counterparts in the Emperor's palace at Peking or the Kaiser's castle in Budapest. Whereas the usurpers of the past cut their way to the top with club, sword or cannon, the dictator of this modern age rises by the glibness of his tongue.

. The Mussolinis, the Hitlers, the Stalins have managed to whip up nations, stir up masses, classes and races, whole continents, by the mere power of the word. They have proven time and time again that the word is mightier than the sword. They have intoxicated themselves and their public with the flow of an immense verbiage and some of it was so dangerous a toxin that in one generation forty million people succumbed. They stirred up brother against brother, nation against nation, and race against race, in order to lift themselves to the top and destroy whoever stood in their way. Deep in the earth of Berlin and Belsen, of Warsaw and Moscow, of Shanghai and Budapest, still lie the bloody remnants of contemporary fratricide.

Hardly more than a hundred years ago three great movements appeared on the intellectual horizons of Europe loudly proclaiming the clarion cry of freedom: the Socialists under the argumentative leadership of Karl Marx; the Syndicalists, with P. J. Proudhon as their dominant light; and the Anarchists who later rallied under Peter Kropotkin. The Marxists, eager to have a state controlled by the proletarians, took over by force all means of production and all property. Their concepts became reality largely through Lenin's cunning use of power during Russia's luckless war with Germany.

Syndicalism, with its unstable project of social reorganization by diversified unions, became a stillborn child of sociology, as did utopian Anarchism.

What became strongly evident, however, even during the formative years of those great social movements, was that the lukewarm Fabian, Communist and Socialist organizations

27

hardened early and completely into brutal regiments commandeered by more or less unscrupulous labor leaders. In fact, a new class of labor leader developed; like those who run Russia, China and their satellites, they have never been laborers.

It may be true that when Proudhon expressed his Rousseauesque aversion to state imperialism he had a touch of true humanitarianism, or that when Karl Marx made the appeal to the proletarians of the world to unite, he too was struck by a spark of goodness. Those who know these two men, their shady lives and vitriolic letters, nevertheless wonder if they were not stimulated more by hatred for the bourgeoisie than by love of mankind.

Both men were violently anti-Semitic, which is most regrettable. Marx, indeed, was born of Jewish parents but nevertheless wrote a book on the Jewish question, damning all Jews as usurers, and their religion as a fraud. He claimed that their only God was money, their religion a desire for it.

It is further significant that a hundred years later three other liberators of the working classes, Hitler, Mussolini and Stalin, made extensive use of Marx's anti-Semitism, which, incidentally, still darkens the Soviet scene.

It doesn't really matter in the final analysis how you rob people of their freedom; you may claim to protect them from a threatening neighbor (the ancient Spartans managed to do that); you may frighten them with the prospect of hell as the consequence of paganism or heresy (as European and Asian priests have done); or you may imbue the people with a fear of Americanism, capitalism or what-have-you in order to bring them into submission to the dictator's aspirations.

Whatever a dictator may want, it is not freedom of the people, because their freedom would mean the end of his power. The ambitions of today's demagogues are just as deeply rooted in the existentialist desire for power, in desire for self-aggrandizement, as Caesar's ambitions of old, or those of the horseman, Attila. And the ruse of an alleged threat from democracies, used by Communist imperialists, has no more reality and substance than Caesar's reference to the Gauls or Hitler's reference to the Poles. The tyrant of today wears, not a golden helmet, a gem-studded crown or tasseled tchakó but rather a simple tunic and a worker's cap.

Perhaps we shall never know the mystery of man's craving

for essential things, such as the feeling of liberty, the aware-ness of this great and harmonious universe or the love for any one of the truly great things that are neither useful nor practical, yet still carry with them an indomitable attraction.

We will not follow the example of the medieval anatomist who took a body apart, piece by piece, in order to find the seat of theology. We are even at a loss for a word to signify this volume of thinking and feeling beyond the practicality of existence, and we stand with sincere admiration in memory of the Hebrew sages, who would not, or could not, find a name proper for Lord, so used a hundred names to circum-scribe his essence. They called him Eternity. They called him the One. They called him the Endless, the Beginning and the End. And how right they were, because the name of God as used by other nations and as used by ourselves has almost lost its meaning; like a coin it wears thin by use and abuse. There is an essence in man beyond mere existence; this essence is the very root of man's creativity. Mysterious in its origin, barring explanation of its purpose, it is yet the only reality in a constantly shifting world of phenomena.

Pangs of Democracy

It would be difficult to trace democracy to its origin. Vestiges of it are to be found in early Hebrew wisdom liter-ature going back four thousand years and more. Our knowl-edge of early antiquity is limited. Much of the documentation available in the great libraries of Alexandria, Jerusalem, Athens and other civilized centers was completely obliterated by the fury of the Romans, and even from the post-Roman period only little has come to us through Hebrew and Arabic translators of the early Middle Ages and the Renaissance. What the Romans overlooked has been destroyed by dominant religious organizations.

Still, from the little we have we can conclude without hesitation that Pericles, in delivering the famous Funeral Oration in the year 431 before our era, was not spouting fancy exaggerations in asserting that Athens was a democracy. In the fullest sense of the word his Athens was a government of the people who enjoyed equality before the law, a law which was of their own making and that rendered equal justice to all regardless of class or origin. His Athens encouraged public discussion and opened its gates to neighbors, countrymen and aliens alike, permitting its citizens the full pursuit of happiness.

Athenian democracy invited its citizens to participate actively in the government, to attend its monthly assemblies, and to serve in their councils and in their courts of law. Every Athenian citizen was expected to be a public official at least once during his lifetime. Athenian government was in the hands of the people, and truly so. It was the people's democracy, where the citizens determined by their direct vote who would hold what office when and where. In the alleged people's democracies of our neighbors east of the Oder, hundreds of millions of citizens, resigned to frustration, are advised from secret chambers of the Kremlin or the Palace of Peking who their next Prime Minister will be, and what unlucky fate has been meted out to the resigning predecessor.

Athenian democracy, like some of the other known, as well as hypothesized, examples of free government, lacked the capacity for endurance, not a defect inherent in its own nature, but one forced upon it by powerful, tyrannical neighbors. In the case of Athens it was the pressure of Sparta that brought democracy to an end.

Because of lack of sufficient documentation, it is impossible to say with any degree of certainty at what time the Spartans turned into the aggressive and warmongering tribe which they are proverbially known to be. It is not even certain whether the spellbinder Lycurgus, who turned a nation of people into a band of marauders, was a man or a myth, and whether his constitution requiring two kings and twenty-eight senators was fact or fiction. The Spartan nobles were organized under a rigid system according to which the land was attended by helots or serfs, who were rightless sharecroppers. The helots were tied to the soil and had to wear recognizable costumes. To watch over them and other bonded men and slaves the nobles created a secret police called the Crypteia. The nobles had divided the land among each other in equal parts. This master class was dedicated to strict discipline with a purely military outlook. There is no doubt that this type of overbearing aristocracy made a strong impression on the young Plato and is responsible for some of the bizarre aspects of his *Republic*. Its dominant position in
30

Greece came to an end under Philip II of Macedonia and his son Alexander.

The purity of Athenian democracy, spoiled by Spartanism, when submitted to Alexandrian pressure, was unable to withstand the powerful military machine of the new conqueror. All Greece fell before the Macedonian, who made the Greeks unequal partners in his conquistadorial enterprises. To secure his rule Alexander assassinated his stepmother and his stepbrother, just as in later years he did not hesitate to execute some of his closest Macedonian generals and advisers. His military astuteness, his ability to raise new armies with victims of the last victory, was incomparable. Alexander left a track of blood from Thebes to the Khyber Pass. Where they did not submit, the towns were destroyed, house by house, and their populations sold into slavery. Those who submitted were reduced to tributaries. His empire stretched for a while from Libya to India; his victims ran into the millions. He married numerous women of Asian royalty to secure his position, and grossly encouraged polygamy among his officers and men. At the peak of his battle successes he demanded that in the temples of Greece he be worshiped as a God, and until his early death this ritual farce was enforced. In June of 323, at the age of thirty-two, he died rather suddenly, having dealt with his own body as recklessly as with those of the people of Asia. In his maniac self-infatuation he had made no provision of any kind for a government after his death; his empire broke apart. He was buried in Alexandria, the city named after him.

Inequitable Equality

Hardly any government marked by whim and zig-zag prejudice has failed to hoist as its true colors the somber principles of equality. However, in a storm the captains of state pull down the flag of equality and raise their true colors, bearing the skull-and-crossbones. By using governmental constitutions and statutes of law one could come to the conclusion that even piratical rulers run the ship according to ancient mariners' precepts of justice and fairness and, of course, equality.

The Greeks learned much more from the Hebrews than is commonly assumed, although the points of contact between

31

these two great people of antiquity have been all but obliterated in the course of time. The Greeks, for example, the Attics, propounded a theory of isonomy, equality before the law. However, they quickly added as an afterthought that isonomy did not apply to bonded people or slaves. It seems that some people were more equal than others even in those times.

The Christian Mother Church leaned heavily toward the concept of the equality of men in Christ. However, the early Church fathers stressed that slaves were more likely to be closer to Christ than the rich because of their obvious opportunity to practice humility, abstinence and a pure life, which would bring them close to the feet of the Lord. In the view of such an attitude, expressed even by men like St. Augustine, it is easy to understand why Christianity contributed little to the freeing of slaves or bonded people, but by concentrating on the good life in the hereafter, tended to accept the bad life in the mere here-and-now as a thorny but quick path to celestial equality.

Martin Luther limited the equality of men, the image of God, to "being in Christ" and strongly resented any transference of equality into social and political life. In his own words, in the world and according to the flesh there exists a great difference and inequality among persons. Such is to be carefully preserved. If a woman should want to be a man, or a son a father, a pupil a teacher, a servant a master, a subject independent, then confusion would be the result among all classes. On the other hand, in Christ, where there are no laws, there is no difference between persons. Thus philosophizes the great reformer. In practical life Martin Luther took a strong stand against the peasants in their desperate revolt for some semblance of equality at the hands of the nobles and kings.

It seems that in the struggle for social justice the evangelists of Christ were always trumpeting to the fighting people "Retreat." It is not until the nineteenth century that we begin to find the Catholic Church and many of the Protestant groups in the camp of the freedom fighters.

Even the American Constitution, perhaps the most expressive document on the equality of man, failed to take into account the very existence of slavery within the borders of the thirteen states—not because Thomas Jefferson failed to write the proper text, but rather because some of the representatives of the South made prudence prevail over justice. It took a hundred years and a million battle casualties to insert that one missing line into the text, and it seems that even after another hundred years a considerable portion of the lawmakers of the land find this line illegible.

While the world west of the Rhine has made telling efforts to establish equality as a basis of society, new ideologies arose right in the heart of Europe and in the heart of Asia as well as Africa, mocking the very idea of isonomy.

A man of our own generation, a paranoiac, malevolent, uneducated Austrian by birth, by sheer cunning and appeal to the worst in man drove seventy million Germans into a frenzy of bestial war dances and a bloody bacchanal of race hatred that made the massacre of the Albigensians or that of St. Bartholomew's Eve look like children's picnics on the lawn. It is noteworthy that the pulsating heart of Hitler's Reich was not to be found among the ignorant peasantry or a war-minded military, but rather in the universities and the highest cultural segments of the German population. By and large, seventy million Germans enthusiastically followed their duly elected leader toward equality and most enthusiastically deprecated, denounced, apprehended and executed six million Jews and a few hundred thousand gypsies in order to preserve the purity and racial equality of their nation. These Jews and gypsies, of whom only a small fraction lived in Germany, were herded together from all four corners of Europe and were scientifically asphyxiated, skillfully bayonetted or machine-gunned after having dug their graves in the manner prescribed and approved in the standard military manuals of the soldier of the new German Reich. Of the executed, close to 800,000 were children under twelve, who were frequently put to death after having had to watch for hours mass executions of the children preceding them. The execution of over six million Jews and gypsies was not carried out by a few hundreds or even a few thousands of Hitler's personal followers, but rather the whole nation participated, including German nationals living in neighboring countries occupied by the National Socialist government.

They all helped, millions of them, by denouncing, apprehending and arresting the unwanted minorities for the sake of the racial equality of the German people. Over a quarter

33

of a million German men and women were employed in the hundreds of concentration camps alone. These men and women visited their home towns and villages regularly on sick leave and vacation leave and were never sworn to any secrecy, as Hitler and his associates were rather proud of these acts of purification and made no efforts themselves to hide them. *Mein Kampf,* the bible of racial equality of pure German stock, expressly, repeatedly, unequivocally contains the plans for the mass executions later carried out, not only in the numerous concentration camps, but also in on-the-spot executions perpetrated by every major unit of the over six million strong active military forces of the German Army. These forces on frequent occasions returned home wounded, or went home tired, and again were never sworn to any secrecy. Intelligence members of the Allied Forces collected an astonishing number of photographs taken from German captors, photographs of executions of Jews and gypsies of all age groups, from children barely two years old to men and women in their eighties and nineties. These souvenirs, frequently showing the smiling faces of participants as well as mere observers, were proudly carried in the rucksacks of German soldiers of all ranks. This is part of the mounting evidence that evil and ambitious men are able to poison the minds of the people with hatred and fear so that at the opportune moment these hating or hate-filled masses can be turned upon alleged enemies to ward off alleged dangers.

The German people were told by the clever Austrian of their racial purity, and that the only way to redeem themselves from the impending threat from the black blood of the Jews was to spill it. Jewish sucklings were crushed to death and Jewish men and women, unarmed and half-starved behind barbed wire, choked to death, and abominable insults and accusations were hurled against the doomed and the dying. Churches between the Oder and the Rhine were crowded with devout worshipers listening to ten thousand vicars of Christ, Protestant and Catholic alike, but hardly a word was said from the pulpit about the unspeakable tortures that stalked the camps of extermination. Not a single minister of Luther's church stood up to give the lie to the monstrous accusations against the Jews. In the same breath did they hail Christ as they hailed Hitler. The shame of the German people is the shame of the German church.

34

Isonomy is evident not only in the early constitution of the Soviet Union, after which the legal structure of Red China is formed, but is also in the Stalin or Revised Constitution. If one reads the Stalin constitution one gains the impression that under this man's rule the people of Russia lived in absolute equality, enjoyed absolute freedom of thought, speech, assembly and movement, that every Soviet citizen walked about with a Bill of Rights in his pocket and was subject to no other restraint but that of public morality and the security of the state. But there is the catch: security of the state and public morality!

Security of the state demands that no one speak or write a sentence that is contrary to the interest of the state. The sole interpreters of what is contrary to the interest of the state are Stalin, the head of the state, and his appointees. Any offense against the security of the state is punishable by exile to a Siberian concentration camp or execution by a shot in the back of the head.

Most offenses against public morals are dealt with in a manner not so very different from that in a capitalist state, but for any offense against the property of the state Siberianization or execution is provided. A man stealing a neighbor's watch or a neighbor's wife will be dealt with rather indifferently. But a man stealing a bag of potatoes from the government warehouse, or a man responsible for damaging government property will be executed. The man who decides what is government property, and to what extent it was damaged, is again the head of the state, Stalin, and all his appointees. That means the Soviet citizen enjoys full equality before the law provided he never utters, or is suspected of uttering, or is denounced for having uttered, a sentence against the party line established by Stalin. A man enjoys complete equality before the law, provided Stalin does not fear that he or his actions may threaten the security of the state of the Soviet Union, or rather, the position of Stalin, the sole and all-powerful interpreter of law and legality, mind and morality of the Soviet Union. At the slightest suspicion of disagreement, or even imagined opposition, Soviet citizens from all ranks of social life were apprehended by the Napoleonic system of *lettres de cachet,* examined in secret trials and executed by the secret police. People who were dominant in the Kremlin one day, were found buried beneath it the next.

Principles of equality were engraved over the gates of the Soviet Halls of Justice; they were engraved upon the original drafts of the constitution, and they were engraved in the books of law supplied to the submissive judges and ambitious heads of law schools. But in the life of the Soviet citizens, equality before the law was nonexistent. Somehow the citizens were made to understand that all crimes could find mitigation, provided they were not against Stalin, his person, his security, his whim and his property, which meant all of Russia. But even abject subservience, of which all Russians became masters during the last forty-five years, was not always a guarantee of safety, because under the Soviet law as interpreted by Stalin and his followers, a man is responsible even for his relatives' offenses. When a boy deserts the army, his parents are Siberianized; when a man appears to have on him the sign of opposition, his children are sent to prison schools or works. Such practices have proven a considerable deterrent to disagreeable activities, and somehow the legal lights subservient to the Kremlin have found ample philosophy in justification of these clauses.

History has shown that some men have succeeded in making all citizens equally poor or equally rightless. But making them equally free is possible only where the interpreters of the law are the people themselves and not an alleged leader speaking for them. The citizens of Red China have been equalized to poverty. They truly possess nothing, not even watch or pen or wife or kin. They live in isolated barracks segregated from their families, mere cogs in the wheels of the commune. They are not free to choose either profession or living quarters. They are not free to express themselves or give any vent to their feelings. They cannot speak their mind or follow their yearnings. They cannot go where they wish, but must go where they are called and when they are called. They are slaves of the state, and as the state is ruled by one man, the citizens of Red China are slaves of Mao Tse-tung. Their status is no different from that of the slaves of Peter or the slaves of Caligula. It is true they enjoy equality before the law. They are equally poor and equally without privileges or protection. All except the hierarchy around Mao. We are back to the old feudalism, with the dominant castle and the serfs tied to the soil, the mines, the workbench.

The names have changed, the places have changed, but the yoke upon the people is the same.

The Wheel of Learning

It stands to reason, that in a world designed for the benefit of one or a few, the education of the many would be no more than part of the general framework of servitude and subservience.

Charlemagne, for instance, the Frankish king who managed to elevate his tribal leadership into a grand mastery of the so-called Holy Roman Empire, regarded education as he eyed the Vatican, as a pillar of an edifice over which he lorded supremely. When he sent out his mercenaries to conquer neighboring lands in the name of the Catholic Church, he dealt with his neighbors in such a bloody and ruthless manner that any resemblance of his aggressive brutality to the gentle homilies of Jesus could only be documented by submissive servants in historiography. The schools he created, to have youngsters trained by monks and clergymen in reading, writing and arithmetic, entwined with the necessary amount of Latin grammar and Catholic liturgy, had a very common purpose, namely, the training of county clerks, tax collectors and traveling representatives whose duty was to inspect, supervise and enforce proper tax payments on the part of the Gauleiter. For the offspring of his knights and other nobles, he ordered training in hunting, fencing, bow-shooting, horseback riding, and lancing. Instead of grammar he provided chess games and guitar-playing.

The educational activities provided by Charlemagne and his successors are reminiscent of Spartan erudition in athletics, soldiering and martial music.

You find throughout history the people remaining utterly illiterate, and literate people using what they know in the service of the one or of the few, and the learned servants rendering to their masters counsel in which the people are properties and not personalities. There have been many despotic friends of pedagogy, such as Peter the Great and Catherine the Courtesan. They all helped to build schools, not for the people, but against the people. Many of the Church leaders, bishops, fanatics, reformers and zealots got the ear of

37

the people and established schools to propagate their particular doctrines. Luther considered the study of the Bible the only important subject; the Jesuits were quite successful in perpetuating scholasticism well into the nineteenth century. For some of them the world began with Aristotle and ended with Thomas Aquinas.

They used the name of the Lord, yet they served not the silent Jesus, but rather the noisy overlords or the wordy churchmen. They taught the youngsters to consider the oppressive prerogatives of the princes as God-ordained. They made free with a lucrative life in the hereafter, making it a sin to wish in the herein for what the palace people possessed, and thus for thousands of years they helped to deflect the fury and frustration of the common man from rebellion into resignation. The ministers of the Church were the handmaidens of the crafty and greedy mansioneers.

Wherever the spirit of freedom prevailed, as in the Athens of Pericles or in the Israel of the Judges, there was free education: education of the people to make them better and to keep them free, not as in the realms of tyranny, where education is organized to keep the citizens misinformed and submissive.

Misinformation comes in great chunks. There are whole cultures of misinformation, such as race anthropology, Fascist historiography and Communist mass hatred. These and other schools of misinformation are grown like pestilential germ cultures in the laboratories of dictatorial schemers.

The race anthropologist who teaches at book length that the African and Asian are his, and of course your, inferiors, is a malodorous and malevolent ugglian, insidious and incompetent and unreliable. He is a High Priest of Hate and served the Caesars to rouse the populace of Rome against the dark-skinned barbarians.

The Fascist historian pontificates in one hundred university classrooms about the world belonging rightly to the Führers, Nordics having been responsible for all great deeds of civilization and literary accomplishments, and Semites best be obliterated. His brand in all known history, from Pharaoh to Hitler, has been in the service of despots driven by fear and greed, roaming the deserts of their minds for a scapegoat. And no sooner have the sands of time covered the ravages these monsters wrought upon an innocent minority, than another obsessed mind comes forward on the horizon, infected with the old disease of bloody hate. At this writing, the shadow of Stalin hangs like a vulture over the tree of Jewish life in Russia. One can hear the growling of the beast searching for a victim in the torment of its insane appetite.

A great deal of light has come upon the Western world in the last hundred years in education as well as in public life. Men like Jean-Jacques Rousseau, Heinrich Pestalozzi and others have risen and given to the people the wisdom and dignity of the mind. Through the blessings of these few, many plains of the Western world have been changed from the hunting grounds of selfish princelings to enlightened places of free, upstanding communities.

But one-half of the world lives still in drab and listless confines governed by ruthless pressures different from those of the feudal era but not less furious. What is ordained as education between the Danube and the Yangtze Rivers is a large and intricate body of malinformation reminiscent of the dark ages and just as malevolent. In the upside-down tutoring, the free citizens of the West are described as terrified slaves eking out a dreary existence under bloody capitalistic brutes; while the comrades of the Red empires—who enjoy neither freedom of speech, assembly, communication nor choice of work; whose very kin are no more than the property of a tyrannically administered state; who are safe from neither arrest, imprisonment nor execution, their future and fate at the whim of a single dictator—these poor and miserable people are given the didactic explanation that they own all the gigantic machinery of which they are but mute spokes in an uncontrollable wheel.

Such is the tragicomedy of education in so much of our world and so much of our time.

The Commodity of Medicine

The history of the art of healing is a sad chronicle of a moneyed profession that was meant to be a service. Being a profession, no matter whether practical proficiently or not, it remained in the pay of the respected ruling classes. The dominant and the small groups around them could buy available healers; the masses of the people, bereft of funds, took whatever comfort they could find in bizarre chemicals peddled by itinerant quacks or in herbs from the woods and meadows prescribed by love and superstition.

The millions of serfs, laborers and slaves who composed the bulk of Europe's population lived through or died of their sicknesses and ailments with benefit of clergy but without the physician, because religion was a public service, whereas medicine was a private luxury of the upper classes. The serf and the laborer had no funds to employ the services of a real physician or to buy prescribed medicine. He lacked even the freedom to leave his work and to travel beyond his employer's estate. In his poverty he was condemned to filth. Whatever facilities for clean living might have been available in his time were not his to use.

Poverty breeds dirt and dirt breeds disease, and the wide masses of Europe in all those thousands of years led their existence in the malodorous drabness and insect-ridden wretchedness of the miserably poor. The people in the palaces and the fine mansions of the trading centers would toss about proverbial expressions such as "He smells like a peasant," or "Dirty as a scullery maid," or "The stench of a slave is upon him."

The stigma of servitude was on manual labor. The nobles wouldn't even carry their sword or a torch at night. They wouldn't saddle a horse, nor would the ladies take a bath, without help of the servant. It was a world of servants: unpaid, unkempt and unclean children of God, destined by man's suppressive measures to live out a life of demeaning themselves and their families, their wives never really theirs, and their children raised in fear and respect so that the few on top might spend their time in gluttony and garishness.

This is not the place to determine or even discuss the extent of erudition of the physicians of the hundreds of years prior to our modern era; the question here is, "Was medical talent and surgical skill available to all or just to the few?" The Hebrews, Greeks and Arabs, from Hippocrates to Avicenna and Maimonides, wrote the texts that dominated medical science up to the seventeenth century. The kings and the nobles used their services, much of which was remarkably proficient. The military leaders employed the surgeons to keep up the morale of the mercenaries. But for the men and women in the fields, in the mines and in the factories, medicine came in the form of a witless brew. And when infection did strike, it would cut down the people family by family because no one provided for them a sane way of living. Plagues and pestilence destroyed one-third of the serfs of Europe in those sinister centuries. The poor of Europe would have perished to a man in these epidemics if not for the inexplicable phenomenon that, as killers go, diseases are more merciful than humans. Diseases tire and die out even without sanitation or medicine. Nature is more merciful in its fury than man in his hatred.

The tragedy is that medicine as a commodity is still with us in many lands. We have more than ten million blind in the world, most of whom have been rendered sightless by diseases for which we have cures and preventatives. Of the two million blind in India 60 per cent were blinded by trachoma and 20 per cent by smallpox. Trachoma and smallpox can both be eliminated wherever they may be. If the despots of Soviet China and Soviet Russia would bury the sword instead of trying to bury America, such a flow of funds could come to the poor that it could wash away most of blindness, malaria, syphilis, tuberculosis and the many other scourges of mankind.

The West has done much to redeem the inequalities of its own sordid past, but the shadows of despotism are rising from the East and threaten the very sun of progress.

The Blight of Slavery

This term was originally a reference to the Slavic tribe of Sklavi or Skleren. The Slavic peoples were held captives by the Germanic conquerors as bonded servants in antiquity and the early medieval ages.

What we commonly call history, what we learn in the formal textbooks in schools of lower as well as higher education, is not the fate and development of the people, but rather chronicles pertaining to the outrages, the scandals, the wars, the collusions, the schemes and the conquests, the treachery, the defeats and the assassinations, the calumny and deceit of ambitious men and women. Such individuals made themselves rulers over territories by cunning or by terror, or remained rulers because their predecessors had provided a continuation of scepter and crown in the hands of their family, such con-

41

tinuation being pompously secured as divine ordainment, laboriously secured as legal inheritance, or arrogantly secured by the sickening prerogatives of the blue-bloods.

The lives and undoings of kings, however, are not true history, but rather its impediment. True history is the life of the people, or, better yet, the story of slavery—because, with very few exceptions indeed, slavery has been the life of the people since time immemorial. And it still is, as these lines are written, in more than half the world.

I venture to say that, excluding a few brief and isolated periods in a few minor countries, the inhabitants of the West and the East up to the end of the eighteenth century (and many beyond that) have lived in abject servitude.

The helots of Sparta, the coloni of Rome, the peasants of Persia, Egypt and Mesopotamia, the villeins of England, the millions of vanquished nations falling under the Roman boot —all (except a tiny controlling minority) lived a genuflecting existence. A true history of the world would have to occupy itself with the fortunes and misfortunes of the kneeling, and not (as it has done in the past) with the victories and tribulations of the enthroned.

By and large, the economies of early and medieval history were based on the manorial system. Until the industrial revolution of the nineteenth century, agriculture, mining and some trading constituted the basis of productive organization. The manor controlled and owned all lands, the forests, the mountainsides and the waters in its territory. The peasantry was tied to the land, one way or another, for the use of which they paid the lord a fee, or fief. In some cases, they had to work as unpaid robots on the lord's personal domain certain days and weeks of the year. For the payment of such dues and labor, these serfs were given the lord's justice as protection, the lord's church as salvation, and the lord's war-making as a compulsory avocation. These above-specified rights (if one may so call them) were solidified by custom and hereditary interpretation, which, among other things, precluded the serfs' children from marrying without the approval of the lord of the manor.

Such was the existence of nine out of ten persons inhabiting the centuries before the American and French Revolutions.

Space does not permit me to discuss the enormous variations of servitude in which the people spent their years. The

42

yoke was heavier in one section and in one era than in another, but fundamentally they were all subjects of a ruler, chattel-mortgaged to low-bending servility. In most cases they were at the mercy of graceless and selfish masters to whom allegiance meant "to heel" at their whip and call. When you see the great palaces of the Roman Augusti, or the majestic pyramids in Egypt, or towering medieval castles with a thousand windows—remember they were erected on the very backs of these stinking serfs and, while the velveted masters gilded their halls with precious works of art, the people of the world were caged in damp caves, windy lean-tos and bug-ridden shacks. In the days of Charlemagne, as in the days of Constantine and Peter of Russia—all of whom were eulogized as "the Great"—you could smell a village a mile away, and all these three great ones put especially stringent measures upon the unhappy villeins.

What wealth and luxury the aristocrats of the past displayed, in close proximity to the miserable wretches on whose backs they were carried! The glory of the old aristocracy was just the other side of the misery of the people, and all the perfumes of the court and castles, the mansions and manors, cannot drive away the stench of poverty and disease that permeated the peasants' and workers' living quarters.

Of course, the lord of the manor was not the real master. The king was the master of all the lands, and he was suzerain over all the vassals. And there were classes of masters—a whole hierarchy of them: squires, knights, baronets, earls, dukes, grand dukes and sundry princes. Everything belonged to the king and was on lease to the vassals, who paid homage to him and swore the oath of fealty and were invested with the absolute power to exploit and discipline their respective domains. Very little land in all those centuries was owned by free individuals in alod or independently. Most of the lands (like all the mines and all the waters) were worked by the peasants, shepherds, fishermen and miners, in one form of servitude or another, with the grand seigneur high on his horse and the laboring man down on his knees.

Even after the American and French Revolutions had broken the back of kingly arrogance, it took another hundred years to eradicate from the Western world the remnants of slavery. There are still people living in our own country who, as small children, saw half-naked humans sold on the same block with cattle and sheep, and at an even later day they could have watched such a melancholy spectacle in Brazil; and you can watch it even today in some Arabic countries where the pattern of tyrannical monstrosity has not changed since the days of the califs.

The history of mankind to which our youth is subjected occupies itself pre-eminently with the military adventures of such paranoid aggressors as Philip and Alexander of Macedonia, Caesar and Trajan of Rome, the Frank Charlemagne, the Mongols Attila and Genghis Khan, the English and French, the Spanish and Portuguese, the Dutch and Swedish monarchs. History tells us little of the people, but much about these puny, fat men with the sullen faces, who were born, or rose to be, tyrants in their own lands, and then set forth upon marauding adventures into neighboring, and even distant lands, on quest of outright robbery, a quest for captives—men, women and children whom they could sell into slavery, be they blacks of Africa or swarthy ones of the Mediterranean Basin, or fair-skinned peasants of Eastern Europe. These kings and princes were forever carrying on battles and struggles for properties never their own, for provinces, kingdoms, marks and other territories which they were determined to add to their holdings. Sometimes they used old claims as the excuse, more often, however, the ancient pretense of an alleged threat and, more often still, there was no pretense at all—just sheer, open-faced greed.

In our youth are implanted the reprehensible battle dates of these kingly marauders, together with the names and biographies of the military henchmen and diplomatic hirelings that have managed to make this peaceable little globe an arena of savage massacre of the innocent.

Because here, too, in these bloody wars of conquest, it is the innocent serf who is sent to the kill for the glory of the grand seigneur—this hapless serf, who has quarreled with none but the good Lord who placed him on an earth drenched with the blood of the innocent and reeking with the gall of the tyrant.

Fifty million blacks lost their lives being hunted by slave traders in the pay of kings and potentates; whole civilizations were obliterated by the navigators of the gold-hungry kings of Spain and Portugal. Who can count the lifeless bodies in the far lands of the world fallen by the bullet or bayonet, cannonball and sword, of the British military, from the days of the murderous Queen Elizabeth (of execution fame), through the gentle, tea-sipping Madame Victoria (Empress of India, no less)?

The tea was pleasant in London, and the court was quiet and clean, but the fields near Calcutta—indeed, the earth of all the continents—were drenched with the blood spilled by the bayonets of the gentle queen.

Our youth memorizes the dates, the places and the *dramatis personae* of the seemingly never-ending mass executions of the guiltless, who expiate their souls for the glory and gain of the guilty.

It is time to make an end to the macabre farce that calls itself history, but is no more than an enumeration of acts of violence and expropriation committed by princely greed and avarice. Let these deeds be dealt with as what they are: acts of criminality; and let such criminality be told as little as is necessary, in admonition of new generations to uphold justice and disavow tyranny. Let history be dedicated to describing clearly and unmistakably the misery that has befallen mankind for ten thousand years, during which it has been held in bondage and misused by cunning usurpers. Let history dwell at length, not on the data connected with princely criminals, but on the tragically few light moments when noble men held the leadership and their fellow citizens lived in dignity and freedom.

Black Cargo

Slavery was indigenous to Asian as well as European civilizations under domination of royal scepters from the Yangtze River to the Nile, and from the Red Sea to the Rhine. Rulers by conquest or so-called legal succession would take citizens and their families from their own ranks, or more often from among the neighboring nations, under flimsy pretexts, by trick or invasion, by kidnap, duress or tribute, and put them under the yoke of servitude, the yoke being the symbol that they were no more than cattle and that they henceforth would be regarded as such. They separated men from their wives, children from their mothers, and used and abused them separately or in groups as you would dispatch heifers in one direction, calves in another, and bulls somewhere else again.

The German peasant, the shepherd from Gaul, the fisherman in Egypt or Carthage, the tradesman of Persia or the artisan of Greece—tomorrow the mailed fist of the Roman mercenary could fall upon his shoulder and he and his kin would be pressed into cages or chain gangs and sold on the markets in the name of the Roman Senate and its people, the ominous Senatus Populusque Romanus—in reality, the Senate and the patricians. The people never had a voice in the government, except an occasional shout for the protection of their own skin.

The slave had no rights or privileges except those granted to him by his master. He could be starved at will, flogged at will, belabored at will, and scourged at will. He could be branded and otherwise molested. Such was the lot of more than half of God's creatures in all the lands living at the feet of a crowned head during the reign of Rameses, during the reign of Caesar, during the reign of Richard or Edward or Henry, and during the reign of Frederick or Peter or Catherine. Take any Rameses, any Caesar, any Richard, any Catherine—the differences were only those of shade, not of principle.

The amazing thing is that the other half of the world, some of whom stole occasional rays from the suns of royalty, did nothing or next to nothing to help the bent and battered, the downtrodden and the bonded, off their knees. Among those who enjoyed considerable benefits at the gilded hands of the rulers—as even they could not live alone and needed entertainment by music, by the poet and by the painter—even among those so tolerated and benefited, there was hardly a gesture, rarely a whisper or the raising of a pitiful eye on behalf of those ragged millions eking out their *vita miserabilis* in the stench of slave alleys and slave galleys.

During all those thousands of years prior to the American and French revolutions, prior to the last few centuries of enlightenment when finally the ocean of resentment swept over the ramparts of entrenched exploiters—during all those thousands of years we had philosophers and literati, bishops and cadis, but one has to search far and wide to find a single magistrate speaking judgment in behalf of the lowly, or a philosopher bending his theorems to uplift the branded.

Only in the lawbooks of the ancient Israelites are to be found traces of equity due the enslaved, and redemption after years of servitude.

Even the great monitors of ancient morality, Plato and Aristotle, pleaded the case of the enslavers and ridiculed those who argued for equity for all men as sophists who wished to make black white and white equal to black.

And how the church misread the mountain sermon of the gentle Jew who said, "Blessed are the poor in heart." Saint Paul exhorted slaves to be content with their station in life. The later Church fathers pacified resentment among the slaves by pointing to it as a consequence of original sin. Bishop Ambrose argued that slaves were blessed with a better opportunity to practice the Christian virtue of humility. Another one, Isidore of Pelusium, pointedly remarked that at the Last Judgment the slave has an advantage over the free man by being able to pass off responsibility for his own sins to his masters. The great Saint Augustine, author of *The City of God*, the book that for a thousand years held up the glory of Rome as above everything worldly, called upon slaves to serve obediently even wicked masters, because their slavery was the result of sin.

Christianity in general made a poor case, if any, against enslavement of pagans or Christians. Somehow it seems as if the Christian churches would rather lean heavily in favor of the ruler than the unruly. Then again, how can one expect those serving by force to act with patience and serenity when freedom finally came to those in chains? That freedom came, not because of Christianity, but rather in spite of it. Christianity has often supported the habit of self-deception. The most infamous of the British slave traders, the later knighted John Hawkins, was of such pious disposition that he named one of his hell ships "Jesus."

Even a thousand years later, the landed clergy of Spain and England, France and Germany, defended slavery, along with all the other arrogations of royalty, as a God-ordained institution. The multiple abuses of feudalism went on for a hundred generations without criticism from the Christian Church. Some of the men of the black cloth even went into apologetics about *jus primae noctis*, the right of the feudal lord to take the bride of any of his serfs for himself on her wedding night. Bede relates in his famous *History* that the English nobles in his time would take any of the serf women for their pleasure whenever they were thus inclined, then sell them at a good price when they became pregnant.

47

The churches in the slave states of America defended slavery almost unanimously, as the churches in America's segregationist states today by and large plead for patience, for understanding, for gradualization—all this in favor, not of those living under a bias, but rather of those practicing discrimination.

Lift the chains gradually, they say, not at once. Let us not cease the humiliation of the black man all at once; that might offend the perpetrators. Let us be understanding of those who cherish the word "nigger," of the judges who never call a Negro "Mister," of the school principals who cannot stomach a dark-hued child in the same room with the lily-whites, of the physicians who feel the Hippocratic oath applies only to Caucasians, and of the saloonkeeper who smashes the glass touched by the lips of a colored person.

Yes, it is for such understanding that these churchmen plead, and how could they preach otherwise? In their own churches, pews are reserved for whites only, and they argue strongly that if God intended no discrimination He would have made the Negro white.

It seems that since the time of Jesus, the Christians have taken His name as a privilege instead of a duty, and somehow they do not cherish the idea of the colored as a member in the club. It is true they send missionaries galore to bring about conversion in Africa, in India, in Australia. They take pride in being benefactors who save the poor black soul, but brothers they do not want to be. If that African, Indian or bushman comes to their town, they would not be seen dead with him in church, in one inn, or even in the same dwelling. They are willing to share God with him in a distant sort of a manner, but not their precious home, or club, or school.

The church's attitude toward slavery represents one of the blackest pages in its history, and has no relation whatever to the teachings of Jesus.

The trading in Negro slaves had been going on for thousands of years in the Middle East and far Asia. The Romans, of course, captured and employed African slaves in the same manner as they imported lions for their circus battles. The modern trade in black slaves was initiated in Portugal in the fifteenth century about the time of Henry the Seafarer. Soon the Spanish followed and, with the conquest of new territories on the American Continent and the need for imported labor due to the frailty of the native element, slave trading became big business in the sixteenth century. Perhaps the most prominent slave trader of that century was Queen Elizabeth, who shared not only in the profits of that particular trade, but also in the general pirating and plundering of the Spanish and the American coast. An outstanding example of her determined seawaymen was John Hawkins, whom the queen awarded a coat of arms for which she subtly chose as his crest a manacled Negro.

At the time of the American Revolution, Thomas Jefferson and Benjamin Rush were eager to include in the Constitution statements regarding the freeing of the slaves. In fact, in the first draft of the Declaration of Independence Jefferson included a strong reprimand of Great Britain as the main and active agent of slave trading, charging King George III with responsibility for the cruel war against human nature. However, this clause was stricken out upon the insistence of the representatives from South Carolina and Georgia, and Jefferson omitted the problem of slavery from the Declaration. Even the Constitution was noncommittal on that point, leaving the issue open. It took another hundred years to resolve it. However, while slaveholding was still tolerated, President Jefferson was fortunate to see the day when slave trading was declared a capital crime, punishable by death. Nevertheless, here again the law was on the books, but until the presidency of Lincoln was not put into effect. Slave traders, even when captured, escaped punishment on numerous technical grounds available to them. In fact, during the presidency of Buchanan slave trading was at its height. As late as 1860 scores of American ships were engaged in this traffic. But with the election of Abraham Lincoln a complete change came about. In the city of New York, on December 20, 1861, Captain Nathaniel Gordon of Portland, Maine, master of the ship *Erie,* was convicted of slave trading. He was sentenced to be hanged in accordance with the statute of 1820. Gordon became the first and the last slave trader in the history of the United States to be convicted and executed in accordance with this new federal law. An appeal to President Lincoln was in vain, and with the execution of Captain Gordon active slave trading in the United States ceased.

The Sheik of Valencia

El Cid, or Mio Seid (Arabic for "Master"), was one of the most colorful military adventurers of eleventh-century Spain. His real name was Rodrigo Diaz de Vivar. He early acquired a knowledge of the Arabic language and Moslem customs. However, the suggestion that he had at one time become a convert to the Moslem faith is bare of confirmation. His diplomatic cunning as well as his military agility were for sale, both these virtues gaining emphasis and renown by his tendency to ruthless cruelty. Some of his biographers felt that his cruelty, which jagged the nerves of even a very indifferent generation, was not spawned in his character, but rather in shrewd calculation designed to develop terror among his enemies, and fear among his friends. If that is what he wanted, he certainly accomplished his purpose. The Moslems and the Christians alike were eager for his services, which were always available to the highest bidder. Alfonso VI, king of Leon, attempted to tie this quick-turning *Campeador* to his court. It is uncertain which was the greater, the king's hatred for the scheming general, or his anxiety over his duplicity.

Among the early heroic deeds of El Cid were the murderous attacks against Alfonso, while in the service of Sancho II, two other sons of King Ferdinand of Castile. Later, El Cid assisted the same Sancho in an effort to rob his sister Urraca of the city of Zamora. During the siege Sancho was assassinated. To what extent El Cid participated in the assassination is not definitely known. However, we find him almost immediately serving Sancho's brother Alfonso, whom only a short while before he had attacked on behalf of the assassinated king. Upon the death of Sancho, Alfonso succeeded to the throne of Castile; he thereupon proceeded to take Galicia from his remaining brother, Garcia. Uncertain, however, of El Cid's loyalty, Alfonso replaced the *Campeador's* officers with his own, and sent him into exile. At this time El Cid hired himself out to the Emir of the tribe of Beni Hud, who, like Sancho, was trying to rob his own brother of his holdings. Here, too, El Cid switched camps and in a sudden dramatic move used an army of mercenaries and malcontents to conquer the rich city of Valencia in 1094. Terrified by the shrewdly publicized terror tactics of El Cid, the citizens surrendered upon the promise of security and civil treatment. For seven days and seven nights the bands of El Cid raged in Valencia, with massacre, rape and sheer vandalism. In 1099 the Moors succeeded finally, after a years long siege, in restoring peace to Valencia and bringing death to the vicious *Campeador*. Hundreds of years later the cadaver of this reckless and pointless fighter was moved from one country to another for a particularly glorious reburial, and the cities of Spain still echo to the sound of epics about this general with the two-edged sword and the two-edged soul.

Friend of the Tiara

Ferdinand V (b.1452, d.1516), King of a united Spain, was named "the Catholic" by Pope Alexander VI (also known as Rodrigo Borgia)—a title carried by the Spanish monarchs ever since. The granting of this unusual title seems understandable considering that one of the children this unusual Pope sired with Madame Vanozza Cattanei married a niece of King Ferdinand. The other children of the Pope were Cesare (also known as "the Phial" for his predilection for poisoning), Giuffre (whose nickname I would rather omit), and dear Lucrezia (the last, but not the least, of the startling figures in this criminal family).

This murderous group of black princes of the sword as well as of the cross inaugurated a chain of conspiratorial warfare with their headquarters in the Lateran. Sometimes the doings of the brood of Rodrigo Borgia, Bishop of Rome, resembled a comic opera, especially on the occasion of All Saints' Eve in 1501 when Alexander and his favorite children, Lucrezia and Cesare, watched a ballet performance given in the Vatican by a select group of Roman courtesans. But other shows they offered to contemporary Europe were of rather more tragic consequence to the life and limb of the people of Italy and France. Even the better elements among the Catholic hierarchy, like the inspired Savonarola, preacher of repentance, had to pay with their lives for opposing infamy and blasphemy.

This Borgia Pope and his predecessor, Innocent VIII, interpreted the gentle precepts of Jesus to the court of Spain.

51

Both Innocent VIII and the Anti-Pope Alexander VI had bought the tiara in one of the typical procedures of simony prevalent for hundreds of years, and both these Vicars of Jesus held a blessing and protective hand over a reinvigorated practice of the Grand Inquisition pompously and bestially carried out in Spain under the patronage of Cardinal Francisco Jiminez, father confessor of Queen Isabella, and Tomás de Torquemada, father confessor to King Ferdinand. These were the men who burned alive in the market places of united Spain nine thousand Jews and innumerable Arabs, whom they contemptuously referred to as "blacks"—the Moors. We don't know the exact number of the hundreds of thousands of people who were robbed of their belongings, holdings and privileges. We do know that they were subjected to the most cruel form of interrogation man has ever known—the ripping of breasts with hot pliers, and of tongues with curved knives. Even the mealy-mouthed historiography of the great band of schoolteachers, trying to whitewash the red of bloody royalism and black popism, cannot entirely hide the horrors of these centuries.

Ferdinand V and his Queen Isabella managed between them to acquire and hold, by war and wit, all the Spanish provinces except Granada. This was the last stronghold of Arabic and Jewish civilization in Spain. The capital city, Granada, was internationally known at that time as a center of art, the sciences, philosophy, literature, architecture, medicine and industry; in fact much of what later was widely acclaimed as the European Renaissance was nothing more than the translation and transference of the cultural wealth of Granada, Cordova and Toledo to semibarbaric Europe. While the riches of Semitic civilization were readily accepted by many European students and scholars, the Semites themselves, and the Arabs as well as the Jews, were being systematically annihilated. Since 1246 the kings of Granada had paid tribute to the Castilian armies threatening their security. But as Ferdinand increased his power and wealth by acquisitions of neighboring territories and by robbing wide masses of the Jewish people, his demands upon the Moors became more impudent, and finally in 1492 he drove the Arab king Boabdil and most of the remaining Semites into Africa. Over one hundred thousand of the Moors accepted the promised charity of the Catholic king, together with the proffered

52

baptism. Very few of them could save their souls from the hot irons of the Inquisitors. The descendants of those few still live in the hills of Granada. Almost all of these Moriscos were exterminated by Ferdinand's successors.

In the same year 1492 Ferdinand and his gentle queen made an end to Arab civilization in Europe, by arranging with the corrupt Bishops of Rome to intensify the Inquisition and make the office of the Inquisition an autonomous organization, the income of which was to be controlled by the king and queen. At no time was any person accused under the Inquisition ever declared innocent, and the property of the accused fell to the Inquisition organization; it became one of the wealthiest corporations of Europe. The Jews and the Arabs were ordered to leave on pain of death, and their property was appropriated by the King and Queen. Those who accepted the blessings of conversion to Catholicism were naturally exempt, but those converts (or Marranos—the Spanish term for "swine") who in their terror adopted Christianity were constantly subjected, especially when they were wealthy, to denunciation and the Inquisition. Thousands of them perished in the dungeons, others under brutal floggings, and the rest were publicly burned. The last of these burnings on the Iberian Peninsula took place in the year of the American Declaration of Independence.

The year 1492 has, in a sense, a·double significance—the discovery of the new continent by Christopher Columbus, and the expulsion and massacre of the Jewish people of Spain. It is a doubtful comfort to know that the money used for the equipment of the ships of Columbus came, not from the mythical sale of Queen Isabella's jewelry, but from the plundering of her Jewish subjects. By robbing the Jews and the Arabs Ferdinand and Isabella became the wealthiest monarchs of Europe, and naturally they used that wealth for further expansion at the expense of France and the cities and provinces of Italy. Perhaps they intended to make the Italians, too, Christians, as they did the Moors and the Jews. They had already, by arrangement with the Borgia Pope, robbed all the religious orders of their holdings and property. The power of this expansionist couple stretched into the south of France and the south of Italy, Sicily and Sardinia, and eventually over the newly acquired possessions in America.

The word "uniting" seems to carry peculiar undertones of

justification. Because unity is a virtue, it almost makes robbery a virtue. Historically speaking, however, these unification processes are no more than willful additions of neighbors' property to one's own unjustly acquired property. Ferdinand the Catholic unified Spain and other Mediterranean territories, just as Titus unified Judea with Rome, or Hitler unified Holland with Germany. It is significant that these three great unifiers gloried in the most revolting massacres of Jewish minorities and drove out or killed some of the most civilized people who came under the power of their sword. Gone are the great temples, academies, libraries and holy places of Jerusalem. Not one was spared by the fury of Titus. Gone are the great palaces of learning, the mosques and synagogues of the Moors and Jews of Spain, their magnificent libraries and museums. Toledo—once called the heartbeat of Europe—is a lifeless, shabby town. All this was done for the sake of greedy members of royalty, trying to accumulate a mountain of gold and continents of land for an insane daughter and other decadent members of their alleged nobility. Who can count the buckets of blood that were drawn from the Inquisition dungeons? Who can count the arrows that were broken in the bodies of the embattled? Who can count the eyes of the blinded, and the heads of the decapitated? And who can count the cries of anguish of those who died at the stake or on the rack, so that these two evil crowned heads and their worthless brood might live in the foul glory of self-aggrandizement?

Terrestrial Pirates

Already in the early years of the Renaissance the semibarbaric European Continent was becoming acquainted, through Latin translations, with Greek, Hebrew and Arabic literature, science and philosophy. At the same time explorers and merchants began to spread knowledge of distant lands and waters in faraway Asia and Africa, with which the Moslem, the Indian and Chinese nations had contact and commerce.

European monarchs who had, for a thousand years and more, lived by aggressive wars and conspiracies against each other's holdings, now spied the opportunity of enriching themselves at the expense of these distant peoples, who according to rumor and travelers' information were ill-armed and ill-prepared against Western sophistication. Spain and Portugal were the two countries in command of the largest and most powerful naval vessels. So sure were they of their inevitable victory that, with the blessings and sage advice of the Bishops of Rome, they divided the unknown worlds among themselves so that there would be no quarrel among the missionaries. What was the mission of these devoted kings? Was it to bring to the faraway primitive natives the delicate teachings of the gentle Jew from Nazareth, with His pleading for goodness toward one's fellow men, humility and equality among all, and for the casting out from the hearts of men hate, violence and oppression?

Sure enough, some men of the cloth went along, and some were not bad men at all, but had they taken confession of their sinister fellow travelers, their minds would have broken in horror and disgust.

The mission of these conquistadors was not to bring the teachings of Christ to the pagans, but to bring gold to the Christian kings, and where there was no gold, to bring the pagans themselves and beat gold out of their freedom.

The Catholic kings of Spain and Portugal, like the Protestant kings and queens of England, had one mission only, and that was one, not of giving, but taking. Where they could not haul gold or silver or furs, they hauled slaves and slaves again.

Exploration, to the princely heads of Renaissance Europe, was not a romantic adventure of enjoying new lands and new people, and the goodness of free intercourse in commerce, in culture and conventions. Discovery, to them, meant finding out where the gold and silver were kept, and where the natives could be trapped like beasts in dugouts or foxes in forests. There was not even honor among the thieves, for when the Spanish and Portuguese had laid their privateering hands on the properties of the Africans and American Indians, Elizabeth, the queen of the pirates, sent her men-of-war to rob the plunderers.

It was only natural that in the long-range projects of marauding navigation, the thieving seafarers would spend a bit of time, men and money on observatories and on the study of chart making, navigation and geography—not too much, but just enough to make the journey safely, to secure their possessions abroad, and to ensure that the booty would reach Europe intact.

The first of these mercenary explorers was Henry, the son of King John I of Portugal. He navigated, not far but effectively, against the Moroccans, whom he decimated at Ceuta in the bloody campaign of 1415. He was the first military campaigner to establish in his arsenal in Africa a school of navigation and geography. The purpose was obvious: more and more discoveries and rediscoveries for the treasury of his kingly father. His arsenal and forts soon acquired, in addition to the classroom, a slave trading post, the first in the Bay of Alguin. And after that came strongboxes for sequestered gold, tied on the very same long chain that secured the slaves. Suddenly the exploration of Africa became highly popular, and vessel after vessel was sent by the Portuguese Crown to the West African coast by order of Prince Henry, euphemistically referred to as "the Navigator." Deeper and deeper into Africa did the learned prince send his armed sailors, who were almost always accompanied by a monk or priest. Thousands of Negroes were torn from their families by the slave hunters, in a new kind of trade in human flesh, inaugurated, together with the theft of gold and precious stones, by this grand master of the Order of Christ. So great was his reputation as a conqueror of the hapless blacks that many foreign kings offered him command over their troops. The kingdom of Portugal, together with the kingdom of Spain, were the last to give up slave hunting and slave kidnapping. By the Treaty of Vienna, signed in 1814, they promised to transport apprehended slaves only south of the Equator. Finally, in 1817, Spain agreed for the price of two million dollars to discontinue slave rustling, and for the price of only one-and-a-half million dollars five years later Portugal agreed to the same. However, for another fifty years Portugal and Brazil continued a clandestine trade in kidnapped blacks.

Among the great slave traders of that time was the Spanish discoverer, Juan Ponce de Leon. To judge by the masses of land, gold and slaves he accumulated, it is doubtful if he had any time left to search for the spring of eternal youth. The greatest riches, however, for the king of Portugal were obtained by Vasco da Gama, who "discovered" the riches of India. These had, in fact, been known to all of the world, both of his own time and of the past. However, what Vasco da Gama did discover, with a score of ships and a thousand men, was a way of getting at this wealth on behalf of his king. In payment for their goods he offered the natives the point of his sword and the sharp edge of his battle ax.

Still another of these explorers was Vasco Nuñez de Balboa, who gave the Pacific Ocean an ill-fitting name. His motive for exploration was a prosaic flight from creditors in Spain and, after years of insubordination and petty quarrels with his co-explorers, he was accused of treason and beheaded.

Perhaps the most ruthless among the hardened conquistadors was Hernando Cortez, the destroyer of old Mexico, who used local strifes to put himself in power and managed to kill the naïve Montezuma, head of the Aztec Empire. Cortez was a treacherous and cruel agent of his Spanish majesty. Like most of the other explorers, he found the King an ungrateful employer. The Spanish conquistadors shared the bitter fate of the pirates of the English Queen's court. They died either in abject poverty, in dungeons or under the ax. The life and doings of the three brothers Pizarro, conquerors for Madrid, read like bad fiction. The leader of this baleful threesome, Francisco Pizarro, was a swineherd. With the shady Diego de Almagro and a fund-raising priest he organized an expedition to the Inca land. The money was to be repaid from Indian gold. Pizarro managed to reach the land of the Incas and to trick King Atahualpa into captivity, demanding a fantastic ransom for his freedom. Upon receipt of the ransom he murdered the king. He also had his partner Almagro executed. He himself, as well as his brother Gonzalo, fell victim to assassination.

Christopher Columbus, the ambitious Italian trader in sugar, had none of the rapacious characteristics of the conquistadors. In his trading he met many navigators and pirates who spoke of islands in the far West. His younger brother worked as a chart maker for the Portuguese slave traders, and wielded considerable influence upon Christopher. Columbus managed finally to sell his plan of getting to the wealth of India via the western sea to Ferdinand and Isabella, whose coffers were filled to the brim by their recent expropriation of the funds of Jewish and Moslem inhabitants of Spain. Fortunate were those, among the men and women of different faiths, who were just driven across the borders and didn't have to face the terror of the Inquisition, and the singe of the *auto-da-fé*. Like some of the other admirals of this king and queen in search of new conquests, Columbus died in poverty and disgrace.

Upon the ugly bleakness created by gold-greedy European monarchs there shines an occasional light of humanity, such as the work and mission of the priest Bartolome de las Casas, justly called the apostle of the Indies. He worked incessantly to improve the lot of the subject people of the Americas, and tried to break by word and plea the misuse of Indian slave labor by Spanish absentee landlords. He is the chief architect of the so-called New Laws, which were adopted in 1542 as protection for the Indians against Spanish abuse. Las Casas' intent was distinguished; the results were insufficient.

The greed of the kings and their affected governing aristocracy could not be constrained, and even after all these centuries, when the kings are gone and with them the governors, there are still classes in Spanish and Portuguese America who look upon the lowly people as having no rights to the wealth of the land which is truly theirs, and no title to the dignity of which they were deprived by foreign conquerors.

The Grand Fagin

While it is said that in the land of Ferdinand V of Aragon, the grand Fagin of the Inquisition, the sun never rose, the subject lands of his grandson and successor, Charles V, a Hapsburg mothered by Juana la Loca ("Crazy Jane"), were so widespread that on his empire the sun never set. Heir to the territories appropriated by his grandfather, the lands of the other unifier, Maximilian I, fell to him and with them the insecure crown as German Emperor—he was the last of his kind to receive it directly from the Pope. But to the east and to the west, to the far north and across the seas, his ravaging troops struck out for more and more territory. Taking advantage of his being allegedly Protector of the Catholic faith, he intervened in behalf of Catholic Reform to split the ranks of the Protestant princes of Germany, and succeeded in using even the religious councils to add countries like the Netherlands to his hereditary properties.

Throughout his life he never ceased to war against France and other neighboring nations, after having bribed the imperial electors with the aid of the German banking houses, Fugger and Welser. In 1521 he fell upon northern Italy, defended by Francis I of France, whom he captured and grossly humiliated. When the king of France repudiated the agreement obtained under duress, with the consent of Pope Clement VII, Charles sent a German army of vandalist troops into Italy, who burnt and plundered the heart city of his so-called holy empire. The Swiss guard defending the Pope was killed almost to the last man. Among those who manned the guns in defense of the Pope was Benvenuto Cellini. The Sacco di Roma will live in history as one of the greatest outrages perpetrated against a defenseless city. In fact, this bloody event signifies the end of the golden era of the Renaissance. The bodies of thousands of tortured civilians lay in the gutters of the burning city. Pope Clement VII himself was captured and held for half a year in a dungeon. To meet the Emperor's demand for ransom, Cellini, who was a prisoner with the Pope, melted down the golden chalices and tiaras of the Vatican. In Rome itself pestilence and starvation decimated the populace. The plundering troops of Charles laid waste not only the city of Rome, but the countryside for fifty miles around.

Charles V extorted huge sums of money from the Pope in exchange for a promise to withdraw the fury of his troops. In spite of the great quantities of gold extorted from the Mexicans, Charles was forever tax hungry, in the Netherlands as well as Spain. He had to ride in with great masses of troops to beat down townsmen and peasants alike who, in despair, opposed his harsh demands upon their earnings. Whatever limited chartered rights ("*fueros*") the Spanish townsmen possessed were brushed aside by this sickly, rheumatic and arthritic little man, son of a lunatic woman and a worthless playboy, possessed by the idea of being the first to rule the whole world. It is difficult to understand the world of that time which threw the reins of a hundred countries into the feeble hands of this broken body with its shifty mind, just because some tricky laws of lien and legacy were imposed upon an utterly confused era—confused by the Church, confused by corrupt courtiers and an opportunistic class of self-seeking nobility.

So utterly devoid of respect for the citizenry was this Hapsburg princeling, so contemptuous of the Cortes and so certain of his divinely ordained prerogatives, that he made the nineteen-year-old boy Guillaume de Croy Archbishop of Toledo. In fact, this prince surrounded himself with a host of personal friends with dubious backgrounds to whom he entrusted the most responsible posts. In later years it became evident that the purpose of these appointments was to make the levy of oppressive taxes easier. They withdrew gold ducats from circulation, raised the rents of all crown lands, and sold high offices for exorbitant prices. In various sections of the holy empire unrest broke out: in the cities of Spain and the Netherlands, in the rural communities of the German provinces; all revolts were put down by the well-endowed forces of the little king. The leader of the Spanish freedom fighters, the heroic *communeros*, Juan de Padilla from Toledo, was no match for the huge and well-armed forces employed by the monarch. He was finally defeated, captured and executed with scores of other rebels in the great massacre of Villalar. And the war of the peasants in Germany, who pleaded relief from the new tithes, the abolition of serfdom, the return of common grazing lands and impartiality of the courts, was put down with indescribable atrocities. One of the most demoralizing factors in this war of the peasantry against a decadent aristocracy was the sharp stand taken against them by Martin Luther. His sermons and letters on behalf of the hired barons helped reduce the peasants of Germany and Austria to the status of serfs, from which they did not rise until the American and French Revolutions.

Perhaps as a sobering afterthought, it might be mentioned that in faraway India was born and lived a contemporary of this devilish Charles V, Guro Nanak, founder of the Sikhs, who opposed the priesthood, opposed the system of caste and false nobility, and preached a great sermon of love of one's fellow men.

Guro Nanak wore a simple cloak, half Hindu and half Moslem, to show that he was both and neither, and that the differences of all religions were only on the outside.

Guro Nanak, too, wanted to reach all the world with his outstretched hands, but unlike the venomous Hapsburg, not to rob them of their freedom and their possessions, but rather to bring them the gift of goodness and the gift of equality. Charles V was the king of greed, and Guro Nanak the prince of humility.

Relics and Lice

Philip II added the kingdom of Portugal to the already immense territories of his father, Charles V. At the death of King Henry of Portugal, Philip's troops simply overran the neighboring lands, brought the Portuguese Cortes to their knees at sword's point, and had the invader proclaimed their ruler. He was equally successful in occupying other territories in the Far East and West, among them the archipelago named after him—the Philippine Islands—where his savagery and cruelty came to the fore in his dealings with the native population.

His brutal regime in the Netherlands brought about a widespread mutiny which, under the leadership of William the Silent, was successful in driving the Spanish from the northern provinces. Typical of Philip's military tactics was the sacking of the city of Antwerp by Spanish troops; in the fury and brutality unleashed against the Protestant men, women and children comparable only to the bloody events at the sack of Rome by his father, Charles V. Europe stood aghast at this and the many other demonstrations of inhumanity manifested by this seemingly all-powerful monarch, who from his gloomy little cabinet at the Escorial, cut off from almost all personal contact with a despised outside world, issued his arrogant edicts, buying the services of some and vindictively punishing others at the slightest evidence of insubordination. His oldest son, Don Carlos, diseased in mind and body, he kept in confinement until his death.

His incessant wars against France, England, the Turks—indeed, on all near as well as faraway fronts—soon depleted his treasury; this in spite of the tremendous influx of gold brought about with the help of his adventurous pirates and "discoverers," and the profits from his African slave trading. Some of his gold and some of his ships, however, were side-tracked, destroyed or captured by the queenly piratess, Elizabeth, who made it a practice to waylay Spanish and Portuguese pirate ships. Perhaps in order to keep Queen Elizabeth's hands off his possessions, he offered her marriage as a bargaining issue, but was rejected. He had previously been married to another English Queen, Mary I, but his presence as well as his administration, which included the restoration

61

of England to the Roman Church, was rather unpopular and he left his Queen Mary by taking French leave. Incidentally, Queen Elizabeth herself offered her deft hand in marriage frequently as a trading point with French and German princes. In an effort to stem British piracy by Sir Francis Drake and other agents of Elizabeth, Philip himself, more a vulture than a dove, equipped a gigantic armada to pay the queen a visit. However, the queen's marauding ships and some fortunate or opportune winds bested and ended the sea power of Spain.

In search of further funds for his shrinking treasury, Philip reverted to the old remedy of religious inquisition against the Arab Christians of Spain, the Moriscos, and against the Jewish Marranos in Portugal. The *autos-da-fé*, the burning alive of these alleged heretics, all over Spain and Portugal, were blistering torches to man's inhumanity to man. Philip sanctimoniously declared it would be better not to reign at all than to reign over heretics. His ceremonial executions of disbelievers at his capital, Valladolid, were the disgust of all Europe, in many parts of which the early glimmers of enlightenment were beginning to be visible. Philip II didn't permit the strangling of the victims of the *autos-da-fé*. He wanted them to feel the full pain of the burning. This barbarism shocked the Turks into a declaration of war, but the military power of Philip overcame them.

Philip II was a calculating man, and the intensified persecution of the descendants of the Moors and the Jews brought him an immense fortune. The exchequer of the Inquisition was in the hands of the clerks of the King, who became the recipient of all property of the Inquisition. The Holy See looked with disfavor and concern on the Spanish champion of Catholicism, suspicious of his motives and aghast at the carnage. In Protestant lands the Spanish Inquisition was used as a powerful weapon of conversion. Paul IV appealed to France for assistance in taming Philip. Philip made war upon the Pope, as he did upon most of his neighbors, and brought the Bishop of Rome to his knees.

The forty-year reign of Philip meant four decades of terror wherever his cold fingers reached out. He lived in morbid isolation, surrounded by crucifixes and pictures of saints. He was keen on watching disbelievers expiating their heretic souls. He frowned upon worldly pleasures, even on essential

62

washing and care of the body. He dwelt at length on the life hereafter, and on the purity of the Christian dogma. He showed love to no one and hate to many. So he died. When his body was found, it was covered with relics and with lice.

The Legacy of Poor Jesus

Christianity is more than a religion. It has spiritual as well as mundane aspects. Its origin is lost in clouds of an uncertain antiquity, as the so-called New Testament, which is basically the only documentation of the life of Christ in its still-extant manuscripts, was written not earlier than the middle of the fourth century A.D. There are only a handful of casual references to the life of Jesus in contemporary writings, such as those of Josephus Flavius with their obvious interpolations, and even those dubious references are available only in latter-day copies.

The best we can say, under those circumstances, is that of the life of Jesus we truly know only that he died.

The Synoptic Gospels and that of John were prepared in the spirit, if not under direction, of a dominant creator. As this very same creation has destroyed almost all nonacceptable and nonaesthetic literature that might have the faintest reference to the life of the Savior, we can hardly wonder that many serious scholars have expressed doubts concerning the very existence of Christ. Even the archaeological findings in old Palestine and in new offer nothing to prove the kind of man who was the Son of Man.

We are, therefore, strongly moved to search for a true picture of Jesus in the only book we have, the New Testament, and on this one book rests the case of Jesus and the case of Christianity. Take this book away and you are left with mythological nothingness.

The New Testament, like the Old, is a conglomerate of writings, some good, some poor, quite poor, some innocuous, some unusually primitive, some philosophical, some didactic, some legendary, some wondrously beautiful.

Much of the ethical contents of the New Testament is no more than direct quotation from the ancient Hebrew wisdom literature, such as the Proverbs and the sayings of Rabbi Jeshu Ben Sirach; such statements as "Love thy neighbor,"

"Love thy enemy," "Cast not the first stone upon the sinner," are verbatim quotes from pre-Talmudic writings. Indeed, aside from the Old Testament and the Talmud, nowhere is so much and so profound Hebraic lore and learning to be found as in the New Testament. I include lore because much of the traditional wisdom surrounding Jesus dates back almost a thousand years prior to his appearance, having had its earlier expression in legends encircling the prophet, Elijahu. As far as the New Testamentary anecdotes of miracle working are concerned, many of these have long been designated by the serious and objective student of church history as typical fakir tales of the ancient Levant.

In this light we see the Jesus of the New Testament as a devout and pious Hebrew given to an ascetic life, filled with love toward his fellow man, with compassion toward suffering, with utter disregard for material things and laws, and moved by the Holy Spirit to bring a new era to the oppressed people of Israel, an era of religious ecstasy and a community of utmost generosity.

It is possible that he may have used the words proclaiming himself King of the Jews. To the Romans, lording over broken Judea, such proclamation was blasphemous against their god Caesar in Rome and this prophetic young Hebrew was crushed under the heel of the Roman dictator as were many of his long-suffering race.

Scarcely one generation later the kinsmen of Jesus rose up in a desperate struggle against their Roman conquerors, only to be annihilated in year-long bitter fighting. Those of them who did not perish in battle or run for the hills were dispersed as slaves into the four corners of the world. The fate of Jesus was not an isolated one; long before His century had passed most of His kinsmen became victims of the Roman sword or slave's yoke. The galleys of the Roman fleet and the cities of Italy and Iberia were filled with the captives of Judea and the fate of the maligned and tortured Jesus was still easier than that of His brothers and sisters who were marched through the Arch of Triumph of Titus, into the dungeons of the circus arena, to be devoured alive by beasts of Africa, brought in by Caesar for the greater pleasure of the citizens of Rome.

When you weep for Jesus, weep more yet for His brothers because their suffering was greater, and the strength that was His was not in them. While He was buried by His people,

64

His brethren were devoured by beasts of prey. Although we do not know how Jesus lived, we do know how He died, and that He died to awaken in man the voice of God, the voice of conscience, the voice of goodness and of tolerance, helpfulness, of those eternal values which the Hebrews called *"Shekinah,"* the Holy Spirit in man.

His cry did not remain in the wilderness; the slaves in the great Roman Empire, the lowly peasants and the lowly freeman, they hearkened to the strong message of this son of Israel. They gathered in secret places, in the catacombs, the cities of the dead—the lusty Roman masters shunned the necropolis—they made up secret signs among each other: the sign of the fish, the sign of the cross, the initial of Christ which is the Greek word for Messiah.

As the days went by and as the centuries went by, the slaves of the Roman world in what is now Scotland to the River Nile, from the Atlas Mountains to the Jordan River, continued their mere existence united in nothing but faith. They had to be dealt with. Some of the Roman Caesars dealt with them like Diocletian, the scourge of the Tiber, while others, like Constantine, known as the Great, dealt with them differently. He won them over, and winning them, he won the empire. Within a few years, during which there were six reigning Augusti:—Galerius, Maximinus, Licinius, Maximianus and Maxentius—Constantine became the sole master of the Roman Empire. This Constantine turned the hopes of Jesus into reality, but what majestic hopes and what monstrous reality.

Constantine made Pope Sylvester the Supreme Pontiff, although he himself treated the Pope no better than a favorite clergyman. Constantine's true estimate of Christianity is easily discernible in his rejection of the idea of baptism for himself, although some enthusiastic historians claim that he accepted the sacraments on his death bed. To Constantine, the act of tolerance toward Christianity was a political maneuver on the grand scale, and from this act of tolerance came an act of supreme inhumanity against everything unchristian.

During his reign of tolerance all temples and academies, all statues and structures, all works of art and literature that were not immediately and directly appropriated by the Catholic Church were obliterated from the face of the earth. Under Constantine's act of tolerance, all the riches of culture

65

and civilization of the great Mediterranean Basin, (insofar as they had not yet been destroyed) were put to the torch by the Roman soldateska and but for the grace of some of the Asian nations none would have escaped the furies of Constantine.

Constantine, the pagan sponsor of Christianity, put his son, Crispus, to death after excruciating tortures, and soon after, his wife, Fausta; and the massacre of his other relatives and political opponents could fill a major scroll. His life was spent in wars of conquest without and within the Roman Empire. If legend is true, that he won his victory in the sign of Jesus, I would say the sign of the Devil would be much more appropriate in this case. Like other tyrants, earlier and later, he moved the capital city to another town. Byzantium, his model, he made into the city named Constantinople. He established a highly organized system of government which served as an example to the pitiful dictator of our generation, Benito Mussolini.

Vicars of Christ

It is with great reluctance that I write some of these things about Christianity and the Vicars of Christ. But they must be said for the sake of historic truth and for the better understanding of the many issues involved here. My reluctance is not born out of the slightest doubt as to the historicity of my statements, but rather out of the feeling that the Catholic Church and Christianity in general at the present time are basically, and steadily, on the path of goodness. Perhaps their present meritorious activities can be better understood by those who have insight into the horrible deviations of the past.

For a thousand years and more the holy city of Rome was the stamping ground of cardinals and other ecclesiastics who might as well have come out of the wrong end of the Purgatory—and, indeed, Dante had them in mind when he wrote his great *Commedia*. There were Popes presiding as Bishops of Rome whose private lives were blacker and bloodier than the most hideous pages of criminal history. In truth, there were some Princes of the Apostles, like Gregory VII, who were men of considerable dedication and learning, and then again there

66

were others who were too weak to fight evil, or too narrow-sighted to see it.

Some of the dreamers among these patriarchs, like Gregory VII, envisioned Rome as the Augustinian *Civitas Dei*, ruling the hearts of men unencumbered by interference from the worldly rulers, and immaculate of sin or corruption; but too many of those who carried the keys of Saint Peter never saw the gates of heaven, as they spent their lives without pause or relief on the very outskirts of hell.

These cardinals and their electorate gouged out their opponents' eyes, sold and bought bishoprics, ordination, indulgences, canonizations, and even the exalted position of the Pontificate itself for money, for privileges and for the favors of mistresses. Even the rosy glass of Professor Pastor, the honeyed biographer of monstrances and monstrosities, must admit that on occasion one could find in the Vatican pleasures usually attributed to bordellos. In one particular instance a very beautiful woman of indifferent morals (Lucrezia Borgia) presided over the Council of Cardinals.

Popes conspired with kings and knaves against Anti-Popes and against the lowly people, and Anti-Popes conspired with upstarts and adventurers against all standards of decency and humanity. Popes initiated the most cruel forms of inquisitorial torture to rob the Jews, Moslems and others professing alleged deviations from the true faith, in order to deprive these unfortunate persons of their properties and privileges. In time such inquisition corporations became the wealthiest organizations in medieval Europe, and in more modern centuries one heard repeated complaints from Catholic inquisitors that there were hardly any more worthwhile objects to be examined; there were only poor fish left in the shallow waters of the Holy See.

The question now arises: what have all the misdeeds of these Vicars of Christ, their torturers' racks, spikes, glowing prongs and singeing torches, their leg crushers and bone breakers, their thumbscrews and tongue cutters, their skinners and eyeball needlers—what have all these macabre instruments of depraved tiara-headed monsters to do with the gentle teachings of the blessed young Jew of Galilee? We do not wish to discuss whether this Jesu ben Joseph, or Jesus of Nazareth, was God-man, *theanthropos* (the name Origen called him), if He was God Incarnate, God Pre-existing, if

He lived in *Homoousia,* in sameness with the Father, or not. I do not wish to discuss any of these finer points of theology. All I should like to point out is that this Son of Man, whom some of the Jews called "Messiah," (which means *Christos*) and others did not—this man, surrounded by thousands of devotional followers, preached a gospel of goodness, of forgiveness, of charity and loving kindness, true to the teachings He himself called the mercy and the guidance of the Mosaic law.

What has Christ's gospel of love in common with the cruelties of Rome's schemingly avaricious clergy?

I cannot leave the subject of the papal rule without giving some of the details that blacken its history. When Pope Paul died in 767, a common mercenary by the name of Constantine was given the tonsure and installed. After two years a group of clergymen under the leadership of Christopher made Stephen III Pope, after gouging out the eyes of Constantine. Pope Stephen III managed a few years later to kill this same Christopher, after taking out *his* eyes. These and other incidents mentioned here are readily verifiable by reference to Mgr. L. Duchesne, *The Beginning of the Temporal Sovereignty of the Popes.*

Gregorovius, in his *History of the City of Rome,* states that in the tenth and eleventh centuries the status of the papacy was appalling. Mistresses made and unmade Pontiffs. Pope Sergius III (formerly the Count of Tusculum) strangled both his predecessors, Leo V and Christophorus. The son of this avaricious Pope Sergius III and the harlot Marozia (the epithet "harlot" was given her by the ecclesiastical historian Baronius) became Pope as John XI. However, he, Pope John XI, and his mother Marozia were both murdered by Marozia's son from an earlier marriage, Alberic II. Alberic's son, John XII, became Pope in 955 at the age of seventeen. The Catholic historian Platina in his book *De Vitiis Pontificum Romanorum* names him as the most pernicious of any of his predecessors, a man debauched with all vices and wickedness. He was undoubtedly one of the basest figures ever to claim succession to Saint Peter. He was thoroughly illiterate, tyrannical, cynical, and had his private bordello in the Lateran. He was given to vicious revenge on his enemies and opponents, and took a particular delight in castrating disobedient clergymen.

Benedict IX, installed in 1032, was only twelve years old

when a clerical collusion made him the sacrosanct head of the Church. He was early corrupted by his promoters. Milman, in his *History of Latin Christianity*, states that this boy ruled like a captain of *banditi* rather than a prelate. His acts of adultery, homicide and downright savagery forbid description. Tiring of confinement in the Lateran, he sold the papacy to Gregory VI. When Gregory VI was deposed, Benedict IX sold the papal tiara again, this time to Clement II. In October, 1047, however, Benedict IX poisoned Clement II, appearing on the scene by simony again. However, he died soon afterward.

The Popes of Avignon in the fourteenth century were of dubious character, given to extortion and simony. The deeds of Urban VI (1378-89) were so repulsive that Catholic historians prefer to consider him insane. Even the cardinals who elected him under extreme pressure recorded him as Anti-Christ. Urban VI had five of the cardinals savagely executed. Pope Alexander VI (1492-1503) was a man of unusual depravity, whose greed for property made him imprison Cardinal Orsino and seize the poor man's wealth. Another cardinal, Michael, he assassinated for a similar purpose. Catholic historians attribute these and many other misdeeds of Alexander VI to the general corruption of the Borgia family, from which he sprang. One of Alexander's successors, Leo X (1513-21), presents a relief in the series of murderous pontiffs by merely being given to corruptive luxuries. He was completely absorbed in the pleasures of the day, in buffoonery and clothing, and bargained for ecclesiastic offices like a trader on the common market. The brazen sale of indulgences brought about the final revolt of Martin Luther during his reign. It is significant that this worthless man and his peddling activities conclude, in a lighter vein, a chapter in history filled with almost unbelievable bestiality, perpetrated by men who pretended to be Vicars of the gentlest prophet of Israel.

Many were the tribunals set up by the Catholic Church in defense of what it called "the preservation of faith," and indescribable is the suffering imposed upon so-called heretics and other persons who drew the displeasure of the Bishop upon themselves. It was Gregory IX, Cardinal Protector of the Franciscan order, the man responsible for the canonization of his friend Francis on July 16, 1228, who inaugurated the Grand Inquisition, the Inquisition which was soon afterward turned over to the Dominican order. The purpose of this Inquisition was to call before its tribunal all Christians suspected of heresy, to question them on their faith and to punish their infidelity. All trials were secret, all judges were part of the hierarchy, endowed with absolute power. All hostile evidence was admissible, all witnesses and accusers remained unknown, no defense by an advocate was permitted, no person was ever acquitted. In the *Documentary History of the Inquisition in the Middle Ages* by Lea not a single case of acquittal can be found. The lightest form of torture to obtain admission of guilt was to chain the accused in dark and watery dungeons for an indefinite number of years. Vidal, in his *Tribunal d'Inquisition de Pamiers,* writes: "Poor wretches are kept in manacles of iron or wood, unable to move, sitting in their own filth upon the cold earth, and they are kept for a long time in these torments, day and night." In Carcassonne the Inquisition prison is intact. Still intact are the stone pillars which had to be carried by the prisoner, and to which he was chained. Most of them would have preferred the short agony of the stake to the long one of dungeoning. Numerous were the apparatus and methods of torture, all of which were decreed and regulated by the Popes, who claimed to represent Christ on earth. You may still see today the rack with its pulleys which lifted the accused by a rope affixed to his hands tied behind his back. There is the torture of the saw slowly descending upon the chest of the victim; there is the water torture, compelling the unfortunate to suffocate by swallowing a wet cloth; there is the slow fire kept under the limbs of the examined. All these agonizing inflictions upon guiltless souls, and many others too disgusting to enumerate in all their distressing variety, were ordained and encouraged, for hundreds of years, by the wanton and fraudulent successors to the Prince of Peace. These deeds of subhuman barbarity, culminating in the *auto-da-fé,* had not only the stamp of approval, but also the blessing of the "unholy See." If we realize that a verdict of guilty implied confiscation of property, we shall perhaps see the major motive for the unbelievable popularity of this abominable form of persecution. Persons who relapsed into heresy were convicted to immurement alive; even burning at the stake was sometimes intensified by the preliminary torture of singeing by straw. Some of the Catholic rulers of Europe, such

70

as Henry II and Francis II, became ardent supporters of Inquisition tribunals, which the people named *"chambres ardentes"* (burning chambers). In the Catholic countries they lasted until the eighteenth century. Napoleon I stopped the Inquisition in Italy in 1808. However, Pope Pius VII reestablished it in 1814 after Napoleon's withdrawal. As late as 1852, for conversion to Protestantism the couple Madiai were condemned in Inquisition to the galley. Under Charles V, in Holland alone 50,000 people became victims of the Inquisition. In Spain the last execution by order of the Inquisitors was carried out in 1781; in Portugal the Inquisition was not discontinued until 1821. If it is true that Jesus sits at the right of His Father, and the Holy Mother next to Him, what words can come in their touching Aramaic at the sight of ten thousands of their kinsmen—many, to be sure, offspring of exiles from Galilee and Jerusalem—burning at the stake and crying out, not for mercy, but for a quick death?

An ocean of holy water cannot wash away the blood of the innocent that is on the hands of those Catholic Popes; a thousand hymns could not drown the shrieks of the innocents tortured at the behest of the gruesome Vicars of the gentle Jew, Jesus.

Crimson Crusades

The exact number of more-or-less organized expeditions to liberate Palestine from the Moslems led by the Knights of the Cross between the eleventh and thirteenth centuries is difficult to determine. The movement took the name from the red cross worn on the right shoulder of the participants in the spirit of the benign Jew of Nazareth, who said, "Whosoever does not bear His cross and come after Me shall not be My disciple." Never has this Master of Peace had such devilish apprentices and never has the name of Christ been so defamed as by the crusading monarchs of Europe. The prophetic message of Jesus to take up His cross of suffering and toleration was heralded in 1095 by Pope Urban II at the Council of Clermont. The appeal of Urban II was a cry for war, as much against the Moslems in Palestine as the Moors on the Iberian Peninsula. The shout "Save Christ" blared out into a bellow, "Kill the Infidels."

The cry to kill has always had a magic effect upon the masses, far more stimulating and agitating than the benediction of Jesus, "Love thy neighbor and love thine enemy." The Crusaders' shouts for war won easily over the still voice of Christ, and the much-desired push toward the Orient began. It continued in a more emphatic manner because many decades before the Council of Clermont, Robert Guiscard, the Norman hetman, and his son Bohemond, who had cut their way through the lands of Italy, were eager to carve out for themselves pieces of the Byzantine Empire; the Byzantine monarch, Alexius I, who helped inspire the crusading impetus, had previously appealed for aid against the Christian Norman invaders to Emperor Henry IV and to the Pope. When they withdrew and the first pillaging armies of the Crusaders appeared, Alexius was more concerned in freeing himself from these bloodthirsty hordes than from the Turkish tribes who threatened Byzantium.

The real motivation of the many feudal lords, kings and knights who took part in one or the other of the Crusades is to be found in the desire to augment their diminishing treasuries with the rich loot expected in the Orient, and with territorial expansion. For instance, Louis IX, for peculiar reasons named "the Pious," king of France, undertook the Seventh Crusade in 1270 against Tunisia of all places, perhaps to recover some lost Christian relics or, as he claimed, to convert the Emir to the teachings of Jesus. In reality, it was in order to conquer Tunisia for his brother, Charles of Sicily.

The startlingly callous attitude of the crusading nobility of Western Europe marauding in Palestine became obvious when, after the capture of Jerusalem in 1099, the so-called Latin Kingdom of Jerusalem was established. This regime ushered in two hundred years of struggle for power. The feudal lords governed the hapless people of the provinces in the same cold and brutal manner as they were accustomed to deal with their own serfs and citizens, and fought as chronically in Jerusalem with their allies as they did against Saracens. In fact, some of the Crusaders, like Raymond of Tripoli even made military alliances, however temporary, with the Moslems. There is no doubt that some of the Moslem defenders, especially Sultan Saladin, carried themselves with considerably more dignity and chivalry than the invaders. It was this Sultan Saladin who brought back literature and learning to

72

a desolated Palestine, after the expulsion of the crusading nobility.

If the desire of the Crusaders was to preserve Christian relics, documents and holy places, it must be said that during the era of their occupation of Jerusalem they displayed hardly any interest in the project, nor did the nobility that led these expeditions have even the reading capacity to understand such matters. In fact, so uncontrolled and barbaric were these Crusaders that their ravages in Hungary, for instance, are proverbial until this very day. During the Second Crusade, which was preached by Bernard of Clairvaux and led by Conrad III of Germany and Louis VII of France, the armies of the Crusaders pillaged the lands of the Christian King Manual I on their trek to the Holy Land. The Church and its various bishops, monks and preachers exhorted the white masses, promising the Crusaders full penance, absolution and whatever else a priest can offer through the benefits of salvation in an alleged war of Christendom for the Sepulcher.

The First Crusade went off to a great start. Loot-minded knights, uncastled barons, impoverished dukes, kings bent on expansion, renegade serfs, adventurers, unemployed mercenaries, criminals with a price on their heads, frustrated lovers and greedy merchantmen, fanatical monks and other lowly clergy, all took up the cross, joining together first in small bands and then under the loose reins of a color-flaunting noble, and set off on the great trek east to Jerusalem to "save Christ"—that was the slogan for more than two hundred years. "But why wait?" asked some, like the monks, Peter of Cluny and Peter the Hermit, and Count Emicho, and the Archbishop of Mayence. "Why wait for the infidels in the Holy Land? We have infidels right here—the Jews." And like a holocaust the man with the red cross on his shoulder fell upon the helpless, unarmed Jews of Europe, offering to history another great example of what bestiality the Christians are capable of in the name of the Jew, Jesus. In rapacious comradeship these Crusaders for the Prince of Love burned Jewish homes, cut the throats of their inhabitants, men, women and children, plundered and murdered from town to town, in France, in Germany, in England, in Spain and throughout the lands. You can tell the road taken by the Crusaders by the marks of devastation left upon the Jewish communities. Hundreds of ancient Jewish settlements in France and Germany, in Bohemia and Austria, in Spain, Italy and England, were simply wiped out. It must be said that a few of the higher clergy, such as Bernard of Clairvaux and Bishop Conrad of Cologne, protested these massacres, but most of the nobility bent on conquest in the Far East were indifferent to these isolated cries for humanity. In the city of York, for instance, the Jewish population was driven into Clifford's Tower and threatened with forced baptism or execution. The whole community perished by voluntary self-slaughter rather than become living victims of their assailants, thus repeating the act of self-sacrifice committed more than a thousand years before by their ancestors under the siege of Rome. More than twelve thousand Jews were massacred in the First Crusade alone. Thousands of others fell victim to the warriors for Christ during their succeeding missions. Many outstanding scholars, scientists and literary figures of Jewry perished in this premature celebration of the devotees of the Sepulcher. The hatred against the Jews extolled by the raving monks engraved itself deeply into the minds of the Europeans, to break out again in its utmost fury only a generation ago. The remaining Jews became wardens of their calculating suzerains, who used them at will, confined them to ghettos, and whenever it pleased their wishes to deflect the wrath of the populace they found in the Jew an ideal scapegoat. It was only after the American and French Revolutions that the Jews of the Western world found their rightful place in society.

The brutality of the Crusaders vented its fury not only against the Jews. During the so-called Fourth Crusade they intervened in the affairs of the Byzantine Emperor Alexius V, and at the conquest of Constantinople in the year 1204, with their typical religious zeal they pillaged and plundered the homes of the Christians, and shared the spoils with the helpful Venetians. Even temples, tombstones and other edifices sacred to peoples of various faiths were despoiled by the Crusaders on their march to rehabilitate the long-lost home of Jesus. Among such acts of desecration was the pulling down of the Mausoleum at Halicarnassus, erected in 353 B.C. by the grieving queen Artemisia in honor and memory of Mausolus, King of Caria. The Knights Hospitalers broke the thirty-six white marble columns of rare beauty, in order to use the building as a fortified castle. It can still be seen today in Bodrum, Turkey.

A few years later we find the Children's Crusade, inspired by Stephen of Cloyes. When the children arrived at Marseilles to embark for the Near East, they were sold by some of the agitators, with the help of the skippers.

The final results of the Crusades were as spurious as their motivations. Whatever holy places and relics of the Church may have been threatened, they are still there until this day, threatened in reality by nothing except the war activities of the Crusaders. The Crusaders left in their wake, during the turbulent era of the holy Latin Kingdom, a row of ungainly castles and fortifications. Culturally they brought back with them to Europe a pack of absurd romances and epics, glorifying the robber barons of that era. However, the impact of Moslem and Byzantine culture upon the barbaric invaders was unavoidable, and some of the light of the Orient fell into even the darkest crevices of medieval Europe. The Venetians and other Mediterranean cities profited greatly by a newly awakened trade, and by the superior knowledge of the Near East.

The two hundred years of crusading brought to the people of Eastern Europe and Western Asia war and devastation at the hands of greedy expansionists, who carried a cross on their shoulders and a devil in their hearts. Along this *via dolorosa,* whose stages are marked by the enslavement of children, the burning of Constantinople and the ravaging of the Balkans, lie tens of thousands of Jewish gravestones—mute evidence of man's inhumanity to man.

The Jews and the Cross

The history of the Jews is the history of human freedom and enslavement. Wherever and whenever the principle of freedom grows stronger, the fate of the Jews improves, and where it declines the suffering of the Jews increases. The Jew has become historically speaking the touchstone of liberty.

Judaism in its origin differed fundamentally from the cults and beliefs of the surrounding kingdoms by recognizing the supremacy of only one ruler whose dictates, as expressed in the Mosaic Code, were absolute obedience to the divine principles of justice and love of one's fellow man.

Kings came late to the people of Israel, and they too had to abide by that principle or be admonished and chastised by bonds of religious discipline. Indeed, a critical study of the book of Chronicles indicates that in Biblical times royal injustice invariably runs parallel with royal apostasy.

In early Israel, the divine protection of social justice extended to all people including strangers, servants and even the cattle.

In order to keep the integrity of the Hebraic ethics unsoiled and undisrupted, the Jewish priests and judges established an intricate system of social separation from Israel's neighboring pagans. Precepts and commandments were placed in the Canon to protect the People of the Book from the people of the Baal. In all the neighboring kingdoms, from Egypt and Tyre to Babylon and the farthest limits of the desert, their respective rulers dominated, not by serving an abstract principle, but rather by devising celestial idols and hierarchies to serve them.

The pagan king was, unlike David or Solomon, the master of the temple, and not a worshiper therein. The king assumed divinity for himself, and that held true for Rameses as well as for Augustus or Ahasuerus. The king was God, the king was Son of God, the king was an object of worship, and his likeness was engraved in stone and paint like that of the other gods. To other kings and their shamans as well as their beclouded subjects, between the Atlas Mountains and the gulf of Persia, the Hebrew manner of faith and obedience to an invisible and unpaintable deity represented a most hateful rebellion against living authority, namely, that of the high and mighty Pharaoh or Caesar.

The Caesars could never forgive the Jews for their obstinate persistence in dedicating, or even sacrificing, their lives, in the service of an abstraction of justice and humanity. When the Jews would rather see their temple destroyed than desecrated by an altar to Caesar, the Roman conquerors were as bewildered as the Assyrians and Babylonians.

When the Israelites finally broke under the incessant blows of the Roman war machines, and were dispersed to all corners of the pagan Empire, the bewilderment of the victors increased as the vanquished, unlike other captives, refused to accept the cults of their masters and quietly but doggedly persisted in their ancient beliefs.

When the gentle preacher of Nazareth began his melancholy trek, teaching the gospel of pure Judaism to all who hearkened to his voice, those who became apostles and evangelists of his preachings were Jews. But when the Romans made an early end to the Son of Man whom His followers called King of the Jews, and whom others called Son of God, the Jews no longer listened; they turned their backs and stayed that way. The Jewish people were weary of men who claimed God as their father; they were weary of tyrants and their claims to Olympian heredity.

Three hundred years later the Emperor Constantine declared belief in Jesus to be the sole religion over the Roman Empire and the Christian Church of Rome to be Catholic, that is, universal. Yet at the same time he declared all Jews living within the borders of Imperial Rome to be outcasts and traitors.

While most nations subjugated by Constantine bowed to his stringent religious edicts, and accepted baptism as they did all their other sufferings, the Jews remained adamant. They did not accept any man as God, no matter how advantageous it would have been to them, to claim their kinship to the prophet Jesus.

The Jews took upon themselves, from the days of the *acts of intolerance* promulgated by Constantine, the heavy burden of persecution and malignment, not because they loved Jesus less, but because they loved God more.

There is hardly any need to describe how the Jews suffered because of their obstinacy on the side of the Lord. No words can paint the bitter pain inflicted upon them by their Christian rulers, and by a people incited by their potentates, religious as well as worldly. The rulers of church and state, in spite of all their differences, agreed to use the Jew as a sacrificial animal whenever the need arose and whenever it so pleased them.

They killed and robbed the Jews during their Crusade. Why bother with pagan booty in the far Orient when booty could be gotten right in the heart of Europe by slaughtering the Jews and plundering their homes? They killed them during the Black Death. The plague troubled the Jews less because of their ritual cleanliness. They killed them during the era of the inquisitors, in order to rob them of their possessions. There never was a reason too flimsy to turn the mob against the Jews, and the Church was silent. The Church was silent when they slaughtered the Jews in the dark ages, again when they massacred the Jews in the decade of Hitlerism, and yet again when Stalin staged his purges in Russia. How could it be otherwise? It was the Church of early Christianity that created the myth of the Jews being the killers of Christ, the Jews from whose midst Jesus arose, as did all his apostles!

But under the three great Christian lawmakers, Constantine, Theodosius and Justinian—euphemistically called "The Just"—the *via dolorosa* was sealed. The theologians of the first five hundred years created the basis, the attitude and the temper for a world of Christians who dealt with the kinfolk of their Messiah as a pack of monsters. This clerical hatred against the Jews reached its height or shall I say depth, in Martin Luther, who demanded that the Jews be made, not serfs, but servants of the Christian serfs, in order to demean them to the ultimate; he even wrote a little book against the Jews which compares in viciousness with such modern literary outpourings of anti-Semitism as Karl Marx's *Problems Regarding the Jewish Question* or Hitler's *Mein Kampf*.

The Christian Church fathers, Athanasius, Cyril, Cyprian, Ambrose, Augustine, to mention just a few, demanded compulsory conversion of the Jews on pain of torture and annihilation. Constantine spoke of the synagogue as a brothel (*conciliabulum*); Theodosius referred to the Jews as beasts and monsters. The worst of the lot was Justinian, who was responsible for codifying the Roman Law. In his *Corpus Juris Civilis*, he re-enacted all anti-Semitic laws from Hadrian to his day, and then completed the act by adding some discriminatory statutes of his own. Jews were not permitted to build synagogues, Jews were not permitted to recite the prayer, "Hear, oh Israel, the Lord is One." In the opinion of Justinian, the Lord was three. Jews who denied the resurrection should be deprived of their property. Somehow it always wound up with robbing the pagans. Mass conversions under the threat of execution were common under Justinian.

The Catholic clergy outdid the Caesarian monsters in their persecution and mockery of the Jews. Saint Chrysostom, Bishop of Constantinople, declared the synagogues to be inhabited by demons. Saint Jerome, the translator of the Bible into Latin with the help of Jewish scholars, expressed the opinion that Satan ruled in the synagogues. Saint Hilary of Poitiers ventured the opinion that the Jews were possessed by filthy demons. Saint Origen admonished his co-religionists to be wary of the Jews because they were responsible for all misfortunes which had befallen Christendom. In the opinion of Eusebius, the Jews crucified a Christian every year on the Easter holiday—of course a different Christian in every town.

When the Crusaders captured Jerusalem they removed their shoes and sang Hosannahs: "Jerusalem, lift up thine eyes and behold thy liberators." And then they went on slaughtering the pagans. They herded all the Jews they could capture into the great synagogue in Jerusalem, and burned them alive.

Thereupon they staged a great procession to the Holy Sepulcher singing, with tears in their eyes and a sob of joy in their throat—"Te Deum."

Oh, my Prince of Peace, Thou blessed Son of Israel, how they have martyred Thy brothers and Thy sisters.

The Fourth Lateran Council of 1215, convened by Pope Innocent III, acted and re-enacted some of the most hostile laws against the Jews. They decreed, among other restrictions, that Jews be compelled to wear a yellow or red badge on the front and back of their coats so that they might be recognized from all sides as infidels. This law was first put into force by Louis the Saint prior to his departure for the Second Crusade. For centuries after the Fourth Lateran Council, the Jews were denied the most elementary rights of state protection and became subject of insults and mockery condoned and encouraged by the Church. For instance, when taking an oath they were required in many places to stand barefoot on the hide of a swine as part of the procedure; this was the old *mos judaicus*. Among the few who raised a voice against this outrage was the distinguished philosopher Roger Bacon. In 1380 Aubriot, the Provost of Paris, who protested the massacre of the Jews, was thrown into prison. Against these few men of distinction and courage pleading for justice and humanity stood a solid wall of Christian barbarism and malevolence. Wild accusations of Jews stabbing the Host, of Jewish ritual murders at Passover time, of Jewish well poisoning, were given public credence and support by the Church. Numerous Jews were apprehended on these charges and put to death under severe torture. As in all cases of persecution of minorities, the Jews were robbed of their earthly possessions. Only Hitler's expropriation of the property of practically all the Jews of Europe comes near the expropriation practiced for over a thousand years by the Church and the nobles against the Jewish infidels. Even those among the Jews who accepted conversion under threat of torture were robbed of all their possessions and reduced to beggary. Some of these new mendicant Christians, by wandering to other lands, managed to get back their faith but never their money.

USURY AND THE PALACE

The legal code of the ancient Hebrews as set down in the Torah emphatically and unequivocally prohibited profiteering by means of loan. This is a precept by which the Jews of antiquity lived, and it was later adopted (Pope Leo I, 443) by the Holy See.

According to Hebrew ethics, a loan was to be an act of Charity, a helpful deed to a neighbor in distress, and should not be planned or projected to the advantage of the lender. It is one of the numerous precepts of the Old Testament based upon the general moral appeal: "Love thy neighbor." The compulsory ample leavings on the harvest field, the liberation of slaves and servants after specified years of performance, the forgiving of debts at set periods, the temporary freedom granted every bonded person and even the working cattle on the Sabbath and other holy days—all these are part of the spirit of "Love thy neighbor" that prevailed among the true believers of the Mosaic faith.

Somehow tendentious history, carefully propagated for its own purposes, managed to depict the Jew—the original opponent of all usury—as its most sinister defender and protagonist. In the early medieval ages, soon after the conquest of England the kings declared the Jews their personal property and while they barred them from ownership of land or participation in common trading or crafts, they used their skill and brightness of mind as clandestine moneylenders to the Crown. The kings used them as sort of a sponge to gather wealth from the townspeople and the nobles, by advancing funds from their treasury through the Jews and collecting exorbitant interest on these funds. In this manner they could easily circumvent the inhibitions of the Church and avoid the natural chagrin of the hard-pressed borrowers, who turned their disdain against the money-lending Jews instead of the Jews' employer.

And in England as well as most of the countries of medieval

Western Europe, whenever it suited the enthroned and en-
nobled usurers, they prompted infuriated masses of the victims
of their hidden chicaneries to vent their hate against the
Jewish scapegoats. The Jews themselves were helpless tools
in the clutches of their almighty masters. These had shut all
the gates to constructive occupations against Jewry, so that
they might make use of the talents of the Oriental exiles in
the service of the court or the castle.

In some cases the lords used the Jews to arrange for loans
on their behalf among other noble heads—shall we say noble
paunches? In the year 1290, for instance, when the Jews were
unable to raise enough funds for Edward I among the nobles
of France and England, the King managed to obtain the
money from the Lombards and in the most cruel manner
expelled the Jews of England from his lands. Hundreds of
them were beaten, mutilated and massacred, and for almost
four hundred years England remained *judenrein*.

In similar manner did the *boyars,* the *shlachtes,* the
dvoryanstvos and the other nobles of Russia and the Balkans
employ Jews of the Exile as moneylenders, agents, managers,
collectors and serf-drivers on their estates. Naturally the
illiterate and ignorant peasant would, in his distress, blame
not the absentee landlord and money lord, but rather the
bearded Oriental who tried to exact his master's demands
from the hard-pressed commoners.

Here, too, whenever it suited the Czar or his governors, or
their nobles with Parisian manners and customs, they would
incite rural and urban mobs to pogroms against the "Jewish
exploiters." Many Communist leaders in modern times, especially Karl Marx, attempting to gain the favors of the white
masses, continued to depict the Jew as a greedy moneylender
and black marketeer, eager for international world power.
From such propaganda the peasant in the Ukraine commune
under Stalin gained a view of his Jewish neighbor that was
not much different from that of the peasant in Czarist times.

This is not the place to discuss the merits or demerits of
the taking of interest on loans. With the rise of trade development in Europe after the Crusades, and certainly with the
beginning of the industrialization of the Western world, interest charges became an integral part of public and private
finance. No Venetian merchant would chance a loan on mer-

81

chandise en route unless he participated not only in the possible misfortune, but also in the fortune, of a ship on the high seas. In those days ships of the desert or ships of the ocean were equally subject to peril and disaster. Lending was risky business, and the lender felt himself more a partner than a banker. The Jewish *Merchant of Venice*, so dramatically portrayed by Shakespeare, was no different from the Christian bankers and merchants on the Rialto. They all gambled on insecure bottoms in perilous waters, and the high interest paid under those circumstances was only an expression of the prevailing insecurity in commerce. The Jewish merchant's insistence upon the life of his ill-fated partner was not based on disagreement in matters of business, but rather born out of an extreme desire to punish the arrogant adversary of his people. And when his adversary gained the upper hand, he and his comrades in collusion acted with a ruthlessness that almost justified the fury of the stilettoed banker. One must bear in mind that neither commerce nor trade could function at any time without the application of interest charges against borrowed funds. No one would lend money to his fellow trader unless he could somehow participate in the profits, and pointing to the Jew as the moneylender was merely an act of diverting stigma from the borrower and of course the Church. The Council at Vienna in 1311 threatened those who lent money at interest with exclusion from the holy sacrament, denial of the right to make a testament, and denial of the right to a church funeral. By shifting the blame for usury to the pagan Jews, all these penalties were evaded.

The Jew as a scapegoat is a study in human duplicity and the power of unabashed propaganda. When the gates of Ghettoism were broken by the American and French Revolutions, the Jews threw off the gilded and silken chains of their masters as quickly as the great mass of the Jewish proletariat streamed to the open fields of liberalism and democracy. There are no Fascists among the Jews, and the Marxist leaders maintain that Communists cannot be Jews and Jews cannot be Communists. To paraphrase a distinguished contemporary historian: to the extent that a Jew is enmeshed in either Fascism or Communism, to that extent is he estranged from Judaism, because Judaism is democracy in its original form— a sentiment repeatedly uttered by Thomas Jefferson.

Wherever we find usury in the historical development of

the Western world practiced by Jews, it was in the impressed service of their noble employers. If usury flourished in bygone centuries, it was not because of Judaism, but in spite of it.

SOCIAL MOVEMENTS AND THE JEWS

The term *"anti-Semitism"* was coined by the German Wilhelm Marr in the year 1880, and the scurrility of it seemed to attract the German mind with the fascination of a rare bird, quickly winging over to Austria, Russia and Rumania—countries that seem to have developed an amazing talent for taking from their great Western neighbor not the broth but rather the scum. In the nineteenth century Germany contributed some of the finest works of true human and humane culture, but along the edges of its magnificent greatness, where philosophy, literature, science and art flourished, there shot up clusters of weeds. These were prickly poisonous and of such adulterate quality that within less than a century the carefully tended beds of culture were almost overgrown with the malodorous barnyard plants. The word "German" deteriorated from a term of esteem into one of opprobrium endangering the whole world, including the better elements of its own people still untouched by the blight of Hitlerism.

Anti-Semitism was ideologically not new, but in Germany it became a political concept, a philosophical entity, a *Weltanschauung*. Reform parties were organized, such as the Deutsche Volksverein, Deutsche Reform Partei, Antisemitische Liga and so forth, that basically had no other program but the humiliation and, if possible, destruction of a tiny Jewish minority in Germany, living to a large extent as professional and small business people. How intense must hate be to have such catastrophic consequences for such a small group of citizens and neighbors, charged with nothing, guilty of no other failing, except a common blood heritage with the man these Christian anti-Semitic organizations refer to as the Son of God.

Scores of congressmen were elected in the Germany of the 1880's and 1890's, running not on a platform but merely on a slogan: *"Pereat Judea."* At the turn of the twentieth century a Mister Lueger was elected Mayor of the city of Vienna on this very slogan, and we have seen in our own days an uncouth house painter grasp the chancellorship, the presidency, indeed absolute leadership over all the Germans of Europe and Austria by means of this enchanting slogan. We have seen seventy million Germans, in the grip of this ill-kempt poseur, pounce upon the Jewish inhabitants of all those parts of Europe over which he wielded control. His multitudinous armies apprehended these defenseless citizens, men, women and children, and put them to death en masse, and in vitriolic violence, by poison gas, by strangulation, by the bayonet and by the club, by freezing, by asphyxiation and by drowning.

It is true that many people who proclaim their anti-Semitic hate feelings and even those who hide them, have no thought of putting these feelings into action. They would rather utter expressions disparaging the Jews as a means of overcoming their own inherent nothingness. It gives their inferiority a lift to feel better than somebody else and, as they have few accomplishments of their own, professional anti-Semitism makes them automatically superior—at least over the Jews. To these walking inferiority complexes anti-Semitism is little more than a bucking-up liquid on the tough road to status. These poor souls fail to understand that racial envy is a poison, and while the parlor anti-Semite is as a rule too cowardly and too dull to carry out the consequences of his hate complex, the hiss of his venom may reach the ears of others, more scheming or more primitive, who, like Hitler, will go ahead and wield an ax instead of the tongue, and point a gun instead of a finger.

The German message of anti-Semitism was propagated a hundred years before Hitler by the Wotan-intoxicated composer Richard Wagner, envious of his more successful Jewish colleagues; and by the inverted student of Hegelian political history, Karl Marx, who claimed that Jewish capitalism was a threat to Communist victory, and that the world had to emancipate itself from the Jews. The message of such people swept across the East and deeply impressed itself upon the poor masses of malgoverned nations and, deeper yet, upon some of their rulers, who, like the Czar of Russia, or the king of Rumania, or the landowner of Poland, saw a ready-made opportunity to make out of the Jew a scapegoat for the order of greed and selfishness dominating their territories. The anti-Semitism of Karl Marx, the son of a convert Jew who wrote in his book *Problems Regarding the Jewish Question* that the

Jews made and unmade kings, that they were striving for a world government dominated by them, that their God was money and their profession usury—this sort of reckless journalism bore great fascination for the impoverished masses of Eastern Europe. It is for a psychologist to explain why Karl Marx found it necessary to fabricate this extensive web of obvious untruths. This man knew from his own personal experience that nine out of ten European Jews eked out a miserable living as tailors, shoemakers, bakers and penny peddlers in Poland, Russia and the other countries of Eastern Europe. He knew that the Jews of North Africa and Asia were living no better, and no worse, than their Arabic neighbors, but were certainly way down on the bottom rung of the ladder of financial success in the capacity of porters, pushcart men and market artisans; that with the exception of a very small minority of accomplished Western Jews in France and England, during his time the people of Israel lived under rigidly confining restrictions.

In Russia at the turn of the century, the anti-Semitic writings of people like Wilhelm Marr, Edouard Drumont, Houston Stewart Chamberlain and others, culminated in an alleged documentary work entitled *Protocols of the Wise Men of Zion*, in which the charges made by Karl Marx and the others are given "evidence." Our contemporary professional anti-Semites have in scholarly objectivity cast aside the protocols as pure figments of the overactive imagination of a zealous comrade, but for many decades the poisonous volume, carefully publicized by the overlords of Europe's East, confused and enraged the impoverished peasantry of these lands against the "devilish" Jews. To the humble Hungarian, Pole, Russian, Rumanian or German peasant, the exploiter was not the absentee Junker or boyar who only rarely visited his castle, but spent his time in Paris or Monte Carlo; to him the exploiter was not this princeling but rather the Jewish peddler or innkeeper, to whom his few kopeks found their way in exchange for merchandise.

We can see now in our days the Marxist rulers of Russia employing the old Czarist tactics in making a scapegoat out of the Jew. If the harvest is bad and husbandry is unsuccessful on the community farms, it is the Jews' fault, claims the Khrushchev press, because the Jews sit up in their synagogues (there are only three open, most poorly attended by a few elderly worshipers) and conspire to rob the Russian people of their agricultural produce. That is why there is no beef in the great Soviet Union, and the reason why shoes are difficult to obtain, and separate apartments are beyond the reach of the worker. This is all because of Jewish black marketeering; furthermore, that the citizen worker has so few and poor consumer goods is due to the intensification of military preparedness because of Jewish espionage and conspiracy with Israel and the United States.

As one can see, the fabrications of anti-Semitic ideology span easily all these decades from Marx to Khrushchev, and from Marx to Stalin. Stalin, however, taking a leaf out of Hitler's book, didn't stop at using the Jew merely as a scapegoat for his economic and political difficulties; he engaged in a steady process of assassination of Jews. Mutual feeling of anti-Semitism formed an early and powerful bond in the Hitler-Stalin alliance, which incidentally was closely adhered to by Stalin. His disastrous defeat at the hands of Hitler's armies, during the first year of the treacherous break between the two scavengers of Europe, is strong proof that Hitler's attack on Russia came as a complete surprise to the Soviet dictator.

But while Stalin learned to spurn his two-timing Nazi allies, he somehow drank too deeply from the spirits of National Socialism. In spite of his sudden disalliance, the anti-Semitic philosophy of Nazism became one of the underlying principles of Stalinism. Stalin even attempted to deport all Jews to Birobidzhan, a Siberian concentration camp, where they would be reduced to a life of serfdom in huge labor compounds. Somehow his need for the not inconsiderable number of Jewish physicists, mathematicians, chemists, physicians and other professionals made the task impracticable, and a timely death put an end to some of the other projects conceived in his fanatical Jew hatred.

The Communist overlords borrowed a page from the text of *Mein Kampf* and Karl Marx's *Judenfrage* by giving the Jews short measure on equality before the law. The Jews in the Soviet Union wear the yellow patch not on their arms but on their passports. The Jews are the only racial group in the Soviet Union required to accept an overprint on all their papers and travel licenses indicating their racial origin. The Kremlin rulers openly state that their schools of higher education have been ordered to accept Jews under a *numerus clausus* only. During the last ten years the Jews have been completely removed from diplomatic service and all other higher governmental positions. While by the admission of the Moscow authorities, over 60 percent of the Soviet citizens are still baptizing their children in churches, and religious ceremonies at Easter time, at Christmas and other occasions are exceedingly popular, the Jews have been strictly prohibited under threat of lifetime incarceration from practicing their own type of baptism, circumcision, confirmation or any religious ritual of their ancient tradition. The temples and synagogues, of which only a few in tourist centers have been left intact, are described in leading newspapers as harbingers of espionage in behalf of the much reviled State of Israel and, of course, also as clandestine meeting places of black marketeers and foreign exchange smugglers. Under such conditions it is natural that these few synagogues are attended by only a score of elderly persons of the Jewish faith. These, in their economic distress, accept a small revenue for occupying the otherwise empty pews, thus representing, together with a government-appointed Rabbi, a loyal front for Jewish religious service in Moscow, Leningrad and Kiev; a front for shameless Communist publicity and an affront to humanity.

The Sultan of Aachen

Publicized during his lifetime and thereafter as the romantic Frankish king with the preferred seat of rule in his beloved German Aachen, Charlemagne was one of the most vicious and bloodthirsty conquerors of the dark ages, forever engaged in conquestorial enterprises and multiple feats of almost childish self-aggrandizement. He demanded at his court that visitors and ambassadors alike fall on their knees before him and kiss his feet.

Taking a page out of the book of Harun-al-Raschid, he set up a regular harem, which included, among sundry females donated by conquered tribes, his very own sister. Nevertheless, he carried with him the key to the grave of Saint Peter, as he considered himself not only the master of a subject Europe, but also the final arbiter of theology, and of Catholicism in particular. Himself an illiterate man, he ordered various councils and conventions to have religious issues interpreted according to his specific wishes. He divided his immense occupied territories, that stretched at times from the North Sea to the Mediterranean and from the Atlantic to the Danube, into gaus, each of them supervised by a gauleiter, or graf—a system closely followed in our time by the late Adolf Hitler. His personal representatives, *Missi Dominici*, endowed by him with great power, were busily engaged in organizing and keeping active the taxes and so-called voluntary donations extracted from his subject people. Vassals who proved indolent or incompetent were summarily eliminated.

This policy of regarding all Europe as his personal domain, and the Church as well as the people as a subservient part of his larger household, placed huge funds of money at his disposal, which Charlemagne used to hire and equip his monstrous mercenary forces. The sanguinary outrages of Charlemagne began rapidly after his accession to the throne of the Franks. After the untimely and sudden death of his brother Carloman, with whom he shared the throne for a short while, he tried to apprehend his brother's widow and her children and made war against the king of the Lombards, to whom they had fled. Confining the defeated monarch, he had himself crowned king of the Lombards. Thereupon, he turned his wrath against the Saxons, ravaging the countryside. As a warning for the Saxons and the other not yet subjugated tribes, this man (whom the Church canonized on the 28th December, 1164) had 4,500 captive Saxons decapitated on the Aller River. Imbued with the spirit that Catholicism was part and parcel of his personal regime, this thoroughly pagan individual compelled all conquered peoples to accept the faith of his church at the point of his bloody sword. Mass conversion rapidly followed his mass executions. He was without doubt the most effective missionary of his era. Tens of thousands of conquered members of Slavic nations were forcibly sold as slaves to the interior of his empire. In fact, the bondage of the Slavs gave coinage to the term "slavery."

Soon after the conversion of the Saxons and others, this self-appointed propagator of the faith struck out south and invaded Spain. By then the terror of his military hordes had demoralized most of Europe and many a tribe submitted to the tyrant without resistance. It stands to reason that an empire of the size of Charlemagne's required trained personnel and troops. Remaining personally untouched by the available cultural riches of preceding centuries, Charlemagne initiated schooling for his officers and clerks in swordsmanship and penmanship, to improve and solidify their service to the court. To attribute to his monstrously tyrannical and sinister government the finer contributions of the Carolingian Renaissance would be like crediting the Czar with the flowering of Russian literature, or Hitler with the awakening of German atomic physics.

Charlemagne made the theory of a Holy Roman Empire reality, but an unholy union this was, held together by the chains of an enslaved Europe. Charlemagne was succeeded by his son Louis, euphemistically called "the Pious." Less than a decade after the death of Charlemagne the chains of the Empire began to break, amid the distasteful struggles for succession by Charlemagne's son and grandsons. The battles of Luegenfeld ("field of lies"), between Louis and his unsavory sons, failed to resolve the issue at hand, the issue which troubled Europe for a thousand years to come: the rule of decadent usurpers over their kinsmen and neighbors—much their betters in all except deceit.

Sunny Mephistopheles

Louis XIV (b.1638, d.1715)

This little man with the great vanity liked to refer to himself as "the Sun King of France." He also engraved under his image the nomen, "Louis le Grand." When some of the nobles pointed out to him that he was bankrupting the state by his personal extravagance he remarked, *"l'Etat c'est moi"* ("I am the state"). He erected the most luxurious palace in Europe near Paris at Versailles, where in virtually every room and niche, including the ladies' powder room, a likeness of him was to be found, either in painting, in Gobelin, as a stone bust or a decorative engraving. His palpable conceit was the laughingstock of European royalty and a cause for grievous anger among the real people of his time. Little did he know that he was overplaying the pose of monarchic arrogance and that the bells already were tolling in the distance for his genus. Even some of the farsighted members of the French nobility, whom the Sun King forced by fiscal maneuvers into complete financial dependence upon the court, joined the freedom fighters of the Fronde, named significantly after the street weapon, the sling. Noncorrupted judges joined the grumbling citizens of Paris in their opposition. However, as often in these cases, lack of unity of command and purpose caused the collapse of the lingering uprising.

Louis XIV undertook to surround himself with industrial and financial experts who were able, by mercantilist expansion and ruthless exploitation of the people, to bring about an astonishing court prosperity—and court prosperity it was. The revenues streamed to the top, but only driblets trickled down to the citizenry. Versailles became the richest court of its time, the envy of its poorer kingly cousins and the kingly focus of the holy fury of subject humanity at large. With all the gold and glitter of that royal Narcissus, thousands of the neighboring townsmen, clothed in rags, existed from hand to mouth.

But in spite of his shrewd advisers and clever ministers, Louis le Grand led his sullen people into a seemingly never-ending chain of conquestorial campaigns. At one time or another he attacked practically all of Europe. He robbed the Dutch of part of Flanders until finally stopped by their "Triple Alliance" with England and Sweden. In the later "Dutch Wars" he gained Franche-Comté. He set up special "Chambers of Reunion" to uncover legal grounds for aggression and, in this manner, he occupied Strasbourg and numerous other cities. In 1688 he attacked Emperor Leopold I, invaded the Empire and devastated the Palatinate. In desperation European powers confirmed the Grand Alliance and finally managed to constrain the sunny warrior. The back of the French tiger was broken and disease, starvation and financial calamity befell his unhappy land. Impotent to continue his military adventures, the frustrated king vented his tyranny upon some of his own subjects. He revoked the Edict of Nantes, a bill of tolerance granted the Protestant Huguenots, driving these deeply religious but non-Catholic Frenchmen out of the country. He employed the dreadful dragonnades, by which a brutal *soldateska*, given to violence, rape, plunder and other abuse, was quartered in the homes of the Calvinists. In similar manner he dealt with the Jansenites and other alleged heretics.

The reckless military adventures of the Sun Monarch, from the attacks upon the Dutch to the struggles for the Spanish rights of succession—the ruthlessness of this pompous and etiquettish, forever benignly smiling, though multiply tricky aggressor on the throne—caused many to wonder and contemplate, and others to fall into a rage of indignation. Alas, that so many misdeeds were permissible, that so much abuse of human life and property should be tolerated just because one powdered and perfumed descendant of just another similar crowned wig claimed divine ordainment to lordship over a whole nation. How terrible that, by the grace of such alleged celestial predestination, this man should lead a million people to brutally cut down their neighbors for his own personal triumph, and then drive twenty million of his own subjects into privation, serfdom and disease so that he might continue to live it up in the glittering castle, a glutton and a *bon vivant!*

Great men arose at that time to lay bare with pen and with spoken word the foulness of that divinely ordained royalty. They called upon the world, and called upon the people to rip the parasitic creatures off the tree of the people's life. Yet in the same century the aristocratic as well as the common mercenaries of the blood-soaked throne of England and the blood-soaked throne of France were driven off their colonial shores by the free states of North America, and driven off the roads of France by the free citizens of the land. In Paris Louis XVI, a perpetuator of the fraudulent divine prerogative of the scepter, paid with his own life for the millions of lives he and the other usurpers had caused to be taken by ax and by sword and by shot.

A new era finally came—at least, new as a beginning of a world to be governed, not by fraudulent pretenders, but by the people themselves and for the people themselves.

With Louis XVI one king went down, and after him many others who tried to purloin the throne of tyranny fell into the dust. Unquestionably, others will try again and others have tried in our time. Only, the Caesarian pretender of this century will sport a marshal's unadorned tunic and a worker's cap, more often than crown and ermine coat, and invoke the name of the proletariat as frequently and with the same assurance as the foul kings did that of the good Lord.

Napoleon Maleparte

Napoleon Bonaparte

It is a melancholy truism: the world buries its friends in the sand and its enemies in a catafalque. Whoever travels through the length and breadth of Western Europe must see evidence of this a thousand times. On the great plazas of Italy, Spain, France, England, Germany and Russia, and the scores of smaller nations, there they are, the tyrants of the past, the evildoers, the burners and strangulators, the stabbers and poisoners, the torturers and lancers, the killers and the maimers, the enslavers and the masters of the dungeons, those who drowned and decapitated, humbled and whipped their own fellow citizens and their neighbors across the river, and across the mountains. There they are, high up on horses of bronze or stone; there they are, in oil and engraved, in the museums, in the schools, in the public buildings—the whole motley array of tyrants and their henchmen and consorts, their courtiers and courtesans, their confessors and connivers, from Caesar to Napoleon, from Caligula to Stalin, from Peter the Cruel to Elizabeth the Virgin.

I have tried in this book to give a small accounting of the great evil these exalted nobles have done to mankind on its bitter road in the five millennia known to us. I have tried to point out some of the misery they brought upon the people. Let no one think that those of their ilk I have omitted were better. It would have only been more of the same, more of the same malevolence from above and more of the same suffering among serfs and townsmen.

None of those leaning their overbearing greed for power and property upon their helpless citizens, no matter how wanton in purpose and conduct, could retain their position without directly or indirectly contributing to the creation or upkeep of certain institutions of learning, the sciences, or even the arts, as increased control requires knowledgeable people in service, and increased wealth stimulates richer and finer forms of entertainment, such as literature and the arts. Even an incorrigible boor like Charlemagne, who never acquired the simple technique of writing the alphabet, flattered himself by copying the Byzantine habit of keeping literary and artistic persons in his stable of servants.

Until the very last few centuries, when enlightenment irresistibly broke through and remained a factor in at least half of the world of today, almost nine out of ten of the inhabitants of this globe were serfs or bonded dependents of overlords. These overlords treated the lands within their dominions as their private property and its citizens as their subjects. They deeded each other these subjects and the lands they dwelled on as if they were their personal chattel. They left them to kin as their heritage, encouraged by a subservient church, by constantly propagandized traditional law, and by silent as well as written arrangements with their participating nobles, and military as well as civil servants.

All this today is known, or should be known, to every thinking person, if not of his own country, at least of the neighboring countries, because so revolting and multiple were the crimes that bloodied Europe, so many were the chains that enslaved Europe, so loud were the cries of the tortured and incarcerated, that neither wind nor water, not even time, could completely eradicate their traces. Still you will find the horrifying images of these ruling monsters, all dressed up and mollified into benign features, glaring from horseback, staring from gilded thrones on walls and ceiling, and looked upon with veneration by young and old as they pass by these monstrous works of art.

You stand at the ruins of the Forum Romanum and look upon the monument of Titus, one of the many arches of triumph, and you hear one of the teachers tell a group of children: "This is in honor of a great Caesar, a great unifier of the Roman Empire, an outstanding general and a distinguished patron of the arts."

And no mention is made that this man Titus, in two years of siege, bled to death a nation that was a thousand miles away from Rome and desired nothing but to be left in peace a nation that refused to establish in its temples altars to the lecherous Caesars of Rome. One million citizens, men, women and children, died of starvation and the plague during this two-year-long siege; another million finally succumbed to the gigantic war machine of Titus. After the storming of Jerusalem, the pearl of the Mediterranean, for thirty days the savage mercenaries of the Romans sacked, plundered, burned and mutilated the defeated. Those they hadn't killed they dragged on slave boats to Rome, to lead these unfortunate victims under the glistening Arch of Triumph. Some of the

93

men were led a few hundred feet further into the subterranean compounds of the arena to be ripped apart by African beasts, others were chained forever to slave workshops or galleys. The children were distributed among patrician households as child slaves, and the women were put on the block and sold to the highest bidders. The high-ranking officers of the defeated armies of Israel, some already so mutilated that they had to be carried, were garroted after the march of triumph, less than a mile away from this monument.

If such monuments are to be retained, they should tell the true story of their origin, so that the coming generations may take heed and be forewarned.

In the city of Paris, in a magnificent edifice reminiscent of one of the great temples, there lies a majestic mausoleum containing the corpse of Napoleon Bonaparte, self-crowned master of France and, for a while, of much of Europe. His way to power is quite similar to that of a modern usurper, Joseph Stalin, who was also given the grace of a magnificent and monumental catafalque. Like Stalin, Napoleon worked constantly and cunningly behind stage, intriguing, maneuvering, manipulating with strings of influence in a highly disorganized society groping for democracy after the breakdown of a decadent kingdom. Napoleon, like Stalin, knew how to reach for positions where the power lay, not where the power appeared; and, like Stalin, he always managed to choose among his co-conspirators men of considerable talent like Talleyrand and Fouché. When the time came, Napoleon didn't hesitate to drive the Parliament of the Five Hundred out of the government with his grenadiers; like Octavianus Augustus, he managed quickly to revise constitution, government and parliament, so that they should become his obedient tools, making himself the first Consul and the only one with a voice and vote. Like Stalin, Napoleon filled key positions in the new government with relatives and personal appointees. When he concentrated on an all-out war of conquest against the neighboring countries, he appointed his stepson Eugène Beauharnais Vice-King of Italy, his brother Joseph King of Naples, his brother Louis King of Holland, his brother-in-law Joachim Murat Duke of Burg, and so forth. His man Fouché organized a secret police responsible to the Consul only. Soon after that Napoleon reintroduced the *lettres de cachet,* which permitted him to arrest and convict any person secretly and
94

without trial—a system copied to the letter by Stalin. Like Hitler, he established an early concordat with the Pope (1801), to break it, of course, on the day he signed. Eight years later Napoleon, by then having endowed himself with the title Kaiser—Caesar—incorporated the territories of the Vatican and kidnaped the protesting Pope to France. In all these years he warred incessantly against all his neighboring countries—England, Russia, Austria, Spain, Portugal, Holland, Prussia—occupying territory after territory, dukedom after dukedom, province after province, making agreements which he broke, alliances with former enemies, and joining enemies against his allies—all in a megalomaniac lust for world power. A mere glance at the lives and works of Stalin and Hitler invites obvious comparison of the similarity in political design by conquest. In his last years of power, in an effort to gain the adherence of enlightened circles for a comeback, Napoleon made a gesture in the direction of liberalism, but Napoleon's experiments in liberalism were little more than acts of political opportunism and carry no weight at all on the scales of justice. Neither does his instruction to reorganize the French Code of Law mean more than an attempt at self-aggrandizement. As he himself said, "I may be forgotten because of my defeats as a general, but my Code will live forever." Every dictator in ancient and modern history has some such constructive or at least neutral deed of accomplishment connected with his name. Hitler had his *Autobahnen,* Mussolini the drying up of the Pontine Marshes, Alexander the popularization of the Greek language, and Stalin the industrialization of Russia.

In examining the life and work of an historic personality we must puncture the darkness of human forgetfulness and see him in the light of his contemporaries.

One hundred million people of Europe suffered from more than a decade of Napoleonic bloodthirsty greed for world conquest. He fell upon villages and towns like Attila or Genghis Khan, burning, pillaging and killing. He brought misery, despair, malady and death to a million innocent inhabitants of the Western Hemisphere. Indeed, this dragon of Mars drove his death-carrying legions as far as Egypt, Turkey and Syria. He murdered the Duke of Enghien in France, as he assassinated the bookdealer Palm of Germany. He, like Stalin, never hesitated to exile or execute those who disagreed or those who competed.

Somehow our historians have lost their feeling for human justice and plain humanity when a successful marauder is called a great military leader instead of what he should be called—a killer at large.

It is astonishing to see a nation as great as France allot a temple in the heart of the city of Paris to a bloodthirsty, self-seeking tyrant like Napoleon, and bedeck it with flags and cockades of freedom on people's holidays—but such is historic forgetfulness, and such is historic confusion, when good men are buried in the sand and the evil in a marble casket.

Hetman in the Palace

William the Conqueror (1027-1087). William the Conqueror, sometimes referred to as "William the Bastard," was the son of Robert II, Duke of Normandy, sometimes called "Robert the Devil." Both men justify a special prayer in the Church services: "From the fury of the Northmen, good Lord deliver us." Having earned his spurs as a fierce battleman in early youth, William set his sights for the great goal of the British Crown, securing the support of the Pope by promising the Bishop of Rome to replace the dominant Anglo-Saxon clergy with more reliable and submissive Italian and French clerics. William raised, in Crusader fashion, a gigantic army of riff-raff and mercenaries, with which in 1066 he fell upon King Harold, duly selected by the British nobility, defeated the king's forces, and assassinated the young monarch at Hastings. From the battlefield he led his motley regiment crisscross through England, burning crops and houses, killing menfolk and cattle, in one of the most savage medieval attempts at genocide.

Having thus pacified the native population, he spent his remaining years in establishing a systematic type of feudalism, on the basis of his infamous Domesday Book, which offered a detailed record of every piece of property in England. If such were possible, his laws and regulations concerning the duties of the villeins and the other common people, and the privileges of the new nobility, were among the most severe in a most severe epoch. From whatever of the old nobility he didn't eliminate, as well as from the new, French-speaking nobility which he introduced, he demanded absolute subservience, establishing the precedent of supreme loyalty to himself, the King, superseding all worldly, as well as ecclesiastical, obligations. He perished through a mishap in one of his many continental acts of military aggression.

William was a typical hetman of the Norsemen that fell upon the south of Europe after the time of Charlemagne. Some of the Norse leaders went as far as lower Italy and Sicily, under the pretext of trying to help the local rulers in their wars with the Byzantines and the Arabs. Indeed, we can see in these shifting expeditions of land-greedy Norsemen the beginning of the awesome Crusades.

The King Without Land

King John (1167-1216). In the face of the almost prototype combination of cruelty, treachery and greed, so common to English royalty, one finds himself with a lack of adjectives befitting King John, nicknamed "Lackland." He betrayed his dying father, Henry II, for the sake of his brother Richard I (euphemistically called "Richard the Lion-Heart"). During his brother's absence on one of the Crusades he conspired against his brother and treacherously endeavored with Philip II of France to prolong Richard's captivity. After the unwanted return of Richard, however, John was forgiven and cunningly obtained the throne upon his brother's death, eliminating the rightful heir, his nephew, Arthur of Brittany. Arthur was captured in an uprising against John, who had him assassinated.

Through his attempts to deprive the clergy of some of their lands, especially the estates of the Primacy of Canterbury, by fraudulent elections, John called down upon himself the wrath of the Bishop of Rome, who promptly excommunicated the King and laid the interdict upon England. John had to yield to the Pope all of England, which was given back to him as a fief; thus he became a vassal of Rome. No longer able, therefore, to dispose of Church property at will, he attempted to recoup his empty treasury by exorbitant demands upon his barons and towns, especially those who refused to join him in his military adventures against France. The hard-pressed merchants and the land holding Church dignitaries united and brought John to his knees. On June 15 of 1215, at Runymede, John set his seal to Magna Carta, the

"Great Charter," which differed from the smaller, previous charters largely only in its size. The original document contains some seventy clauses, of which very few specified protection of the villeins and the common people. Almost all the text is written to secure the feudal rights and privileges of the barons, with some provisions made concerning the inviolability of the Catholic Church, and the trading rights of London and other towns.

It was not till many centuries later that some of the vague wording of Magna Carta was interpreted as a guarantee of *habeas corpus* and trial by jury. By no means is such interpretation open and implicit in the original charter.

Incidentally, not only John, but for hundreds of years all the succeeding monarchs of England, repudiated the alleged basic grants. The very year after the charter was signed, civil war made all too evident the ineffectiveness of the document. Protagonists of parliamentary rule, such as Sir Edward Coke as early as the seventeenth century, endeavored by daring interpretation to find in the charter the principle of prohibition of taxation without representation, and also a guarantee of the fundamental rights of the House of Commons. However, Magna Carta had little practical effect in controlling the tyrannical and overbearing powers of the British monarchs. The concept of limitation of Crown power may be somewhere inherent in a few of its clauses, but the people of England saw little evidence of such clauses until the postrevolutionary era of enlightenment, when the royal upper crust crumbled on the European Continent, and historians were free to philosophize about early evidence of liberal thought.

Wat Tyler

Wat Tyler, as he was commonly called, was one of the most outstanding figures of medieval Britain. Still, because of the type of historiography that is being practiced, hardly anything of importance has been recorded about the origin and the early background of this truly great man. Some have referred to him as the Spartacus of England, but Wat Tyler was much more than that. Spartacus and his cohorts represented an intrinsically aimless, but heroic, effort of protest against patrician arrogance and the cruel way of life of Caesarian Rome, while Tyler's rebellion (and a roof tiler he was) grew out of the same spirit of frustration of the little man against the nobility, and especially The Crown. But Tyler's movement against the suppressing authorities was a popular one, engulfing the wide streams of England's wretched villeins and bonded tenants, as well as the growing number of cities' laboring classes.

The Black Death of the middle-fourteenth century had robbed the island, and especially the towns, of more than one-third of the laboring population. It was the first time in hundreds of years that hands of the working man, the artisan as well as the peasant, were not raised in the gesture of begging and submission, but stood still in a silent demand for honorable compensation and treatment with dignity. The want of labor was greater than the want of bread, and labor had its day. The Crown's response to the pleading of the lower classes for decency and dignity was the infamous Statute of Laborers (1351), published over the signature of King Edward III (1312-1377). This Prince of Windsor, whose reign was dominated by the Hundred Years' War with the French, and his attacks against the Scots, in a seemingly endless struggle over his foreign holdings, following the examples of his predecessors, enriched the empty coffers of his treasury at the expense of church revenues and, of course, the common man. The greed of Edward of Windsor was inflamed by his mistress, the cunning Alice Perrers, and his brood of rivaling sons, especially John of Gaunt.

The Statute of Laborers was designed to limit wages to the pittance customary prior to the ravages of the Black Death, and prescribed severe punishment for the offense of demanding a fair wage. In the years to come, in the reign of Richard II, grandson of this Edward III and the last sovereign among Edward's descendants, the boy grandson and his uncles, the Black Princes, placed an additional head tax on the people of the land. They restricted the cities in their municipal liberties, and increased (if such were possible) the rigidity of the Grand Seigneur system under which the peasants led their wretched serf existence. The feudal services required of the villeins became more severe and extensive. The sale of some of the basic trade goods was monopolized to cover lavish expenditures at the palaces, and the purchase of certain goods was restricted to the gentry, doubtful recompense indeed.

Punishment for any infraction of the statutes and new laws of the warring princes was most severe. The dungeons in the Tower were filled with the sighs of the chained, heads rolled in the sand of the courtyard, justice was meted out by corrupt officials, and the good rules of Parliament were more ignored than obeyed.

In these days of unmitigated shame and suppression rose this man Wat Tyler and his growing bands of the dedicated: poor priests, desperate peasants, and hopeless day laborers from London town. It was the first time that terror rose no longer in the hearts of the suppressed, but in those of the cold and brutal nobility of England. Prisoners were liberated, malevolent officials destroyed, and some of the haughty mansions put to the torch. The boy king, cleverly advised, met the ragged troops of Wat Tyler at Mile End, and granted privileges to the people. But all this was only a ruse to gain time and at the next meeting Wat Tyler, after severe provocation, was mortally wounded by the Mayor of London; and the bewildered masses, deprived of their leader, gave up their cause as lost, and lost indeed it was. The great revolt was crushed in the blood of the poor, and England remained a land of serfs and noblemen for hundreds of years to come.

The grants of Mile End did as little to remove the yoke from the shoulders of the working classes as did the Magna Carta to close the dungeons or break the chains of the indentured.

The name of Wat Tyler will live on in the history of the people of England, in all freedom-loving men, long after the names and titles of the vicious little crowned heads, their sycophantic and intriguing aristocracy, with the places and dates of their respective battles and assassinations, will have been forgotten, because indeed all this belongs in the pages, not of history, but of criminology.

There were many who lent Tyler a helping hand, and took up the cudgels against tyranny. Among the many was the hedge priest, John Ball, who, like Wycliffe, sermonized to bring the Bible to the common man and establish in the country a new social order based on legal Biblism. Much of what Father John Ball wrote and sang has been forgotten by an ungrateful history. He touched the people's heart with
100

such verses as "When Adam delved and Eve span, who was then the gentleman?" Father Ball was one of the prisoners liberated by Tyler in his campaign. After the treachery of Mile End, Father Ball breathed out his divine soul in King Richard's torture chamber. He was drawn and quartered.

TILLERS OF ALIEN LANDS

It is difficult to describe in a few words the system of social operation that was prevalent in England at the time of the Peasant Revolt—a system that drove men like Wat Tyler and Jack Straw to open rebellion. The most salient feature of the peasants' lot was, first of all, complete rightlessness before the law. Villein or tenant, vagrant or handyman, servant or yeoman—all were subject to the absolute jurisdiction of the manorial court where the will and wish of the noble or his bailiff were decisive. The peasant in particular was subject to the poll tax, to his daughter's marriage tax, and to any other demands his sovereign decided to impose.

Although his kin may have lived on the land for hundreds of years, none of it was his: the brooks were not his and the forests were forbidden to him; the lord could jail him on mere suspicion of any crime against "vert or venison" (wood or game). It was the law that deprived him of all property rights; it was the law that chained him to the land; and it was the law that penalized him with taxes for merely existing. The taxes collected were never used for him, but often against him. It was the law that prohibited even more liberal employers from raising his wages, held at a minimum. It was the very outrage of the law that drove the peasants to revolt against the petty local oppressors. The reeves and bailiffs of the landlords, the haughty clerks and tax collectors of the rich and, last but not least, the heartless bishops who, landowners themselves, perpetrated injustice as freely as the secular lieges. Much touching sentiment against this revolting setup, typical of almost all of the Western world in these thousands of years, is to be found in the stories about Robin Hood, the hero of a downtrodden peasantry. Like many truly great deeds in history, deeds of liberation and enlightenment, the Peasants' Revolt began with dreams and with legends,

101

but even as early as the era of Robin Hood there were knowledgeable men who foresaw the inevitable doom of ignobility and ignominy.

The Opulent Plunderer

Henry VIII (1491-1547), rightful successor to the throne of England, was endowed with all the attributes of a medieval British Sovereign of the Realm. He was cruel, ruthless, heartless and ambitious. He is often referred to as the Defender of the Faith, a title bestowed upon him by the Pope as a prize for the essay directed against Luther entitled *"Adsertio Septem Sacramentorum,"* which pamphlet bears the unmistakable stamp of the penmanship of Sir Thomas More. His private life was animated by six official marriages and bluebeard type assassinations of various wives, the grimness of which would sicken the imagination. Henry VIII was obsessed with the desire to display an opulent continental court in poor old London. He gloried in Parisian type banquets and medieval-type fancy dress, and somehow established, in a clumsy way, a synthetic bit of artistic and literary Florence and Venice on the Thames.

In spite of the shrewd administrative talents of his Lord Chancellor, Thomas Wolsey, the gluttonous king was unable to secure the necessary funds, through the usual taxation. Having already weakened and bled the nobility, and through them the common man, he conceived the notion of reimbursing his dwindling treasury at the expense of the Church. Using as pretext the refusal of the Pope to sanction his divorce from Katherine of Aragon, he fell upon the monasteries and other Church properties, and appropriated them for the Crown, using in this process a fanciful theological rationalization readily supplied to him by such men as Thomas Cranmer, who later became Archbishop of Canterbury, and Thomas Cromwell, whom the King finally made Lord Chamberlain. Cranmer and Cromwell were the helpful architects of the King's act of supremacy, his expropriation of the Church's properties as well as those of some of the wealthier of the English nobility, and although neither of them ever ceased in their attempts to whitewash the King's bloody marriage bed, they too fell victims to the executioner's ax, which, one might say, was almost as essential to the British monarchy as the crown and scepter.

While a few of the Kings and Queens in the hundreds of years following this monstrous Henry VIII defended the Pope, though most preferred the wild monk of Germany, the Kings of England and their Queens as well, had a rare predilection for cutting off the heads of statesmen and clergy alike, and an uncontrollable intent to burn at the stake dissidents or former courtiers.

In spite of his political naïveté, Henry VIII was a master in packing Parliament with his own personal clerical hierarchy and King's officers. Only a very superficial observer could fail to detect the sham of pseudo-democratic procedure and popular support that appeared on the surface of Renaissance England, or the underlying truth, that the whole political and legal structure was cleverly directed by this wanton Lord of the Tower. Henry VIII's military adventures were varied, and his alliances as unstable as his marriages. He would one day swear loyalty to the Emperor of the Holy Roman Empire against France, and the very next day, to the King of France against the Emperor.

Indefatigable Virgin

Elizabeth I (1533-1603). Like her predecessors, this Virgin Queen continued with the help of a tightly controlled nobility to reign over England as her personal domain, involving the villeins and the other small people alike in endless wars of aggression over additional or endangered Crown property. The mastermind behind her policy of Crown aggrandizement was Baron William Cecil Burghley, the man behind the ax that severed the head of Mary Queen of Scotland, who for decades posed a threat to Elizabeth's succession to the English throne.

Politically speaking, Queen Elizabeth's strongest weapons during her 45 years of oppression were her navy and her virginity. In times of diplomatic frustration the latter was offered to numerous heads, among them the French princes of Anjou and Alençon, and the Austrian Archduke Charles.

Whenever her Parliament—the "her" is emphasized—suggested a suitable marriage, she vowed to die a virgin queen; well, a queen she died, the last of the murderous clan of Tudor.

The chain of Queen Elizabeth's lovers certainly sets a record in length and depravity. Many of her paramours died in the Tower; others, like Essex, under the ax, with the mistress signing the death warrant. Essex's quarrels with another favorite of the London Messalina, Sir Walter Raleigh, are of comic opera vintage.

Like most of the Queen's boudoir cabinet, Essex was an adventurer with military talents, not without cultural and artistic graces, ready to serve the lady in expanding her empire.

Another lover of the spinster was Sir Christopher Hatton, who is said to have drawn the lady's attention to himself by his graceful dancing at court affairs. He became Lord Chancellor. Some beautiful gardens near London were touchingly named after him.

Another in the Queen's personal entourage was the Earl of Leicester, master of the lady's horses. His wife died under mysterious circumstances the year he got closer access to Her Majesty, but no case was made. The rascal, however, married bigamously in 1573 and 1578, which quite disturbed his palace status. He was a great favorite with the acting profession of his time.

Perhaps the most colorful of the Apollo brigade was Sir Walter Raleigh, who was granted by the Queen huge estates after a rather sudden acquaintanceship. Sir Walter delighted in adventurous expeditions but, like many others, found his way into a prison cell in the Tower over an infatuation with Elizabeth Throckmorton, one of the Queen's maids of honor. Set free, he engaged in a bohemian life of literary activity combined with piratous adventures on the high seas. He was executed by the Queen's successor, King James I, the son of Mary of Scotland. This son ingratiated himself with Elizabeth by making light, very light indeed, of his mother's execution.

Not all the Queen's mariners were boudoir intimates. There was Sir John Hawkins, the spiritual father of England's slave trade. He learned to appreciate the blacks as merchandise. He captured Negroes on the African coast and sold them in Spanish ports; he even pirated slaves from Portuguese ships and peddled them along the Spanish Main. All this was done with the knowledge and connivance of the court, which rewarded him with the office of Treasurer of the Navy.

Another pirate in the service of a grateful Queen was Sir Francis Drake. He got his training as captain on one of the slave-hunting ships of his kinsman, Sir John Hawkins.

In 1572 he began officially his pirating expeditions against Spanish shipping. He reached Panama, where his wild crew burned and looted Spanish towns. Upon his return with immense amounts of silver the Queen appointed him commander of the naval forces against Ireland.

While Elizabeth played coy marriage candidate with Philip of Spain, her Admiral Drake raided the Spanish ports and ships. Drake sailed far and wide and by his piracy made the Queen wealthy beyond all expectations. Finally, all pretense was dropped and Drake was openly knighted.

Now placed in charge of a great English fleet, Drake made his grand tour of pillage which carried him from Vigo in Spain to the Florida coast. Not a town in Florida was spurned by the mercenaries. He was an admiral in the fleet and he later helped the winds to destroy the Spanish armada.

In addition to sicking her pirates and paramours against the Spanish, the Queen ordered three different invasions of Catholic Ireland, during which the villages and towns of the devout inhabitants were pillaged and burned by mercenaries. The Irish were excluded from all civic life and a severe penal code was enforced against all Catholics.

With Elizabeth begins England's policy of colonial oppression, slave trading and vassalization of weaker nations. It reached its height under the able Queen Victoria.

The simultaneous activities of men of arts, philosophy, science and literature are attributable to the renaissance that came upon the Western world with the revival of the ancient greatness of Greek, Hebrew and Asian civilizations. The lustful and power-greedy Queen had as little a hand in it as the Czar in the making of Tolstoy and Dostoyevski, or Hitler in the making of Albert Einstein. The wonder of creativity occurs in spite of tyranny and not because of it.

The Horrible Hanoverians

For better than a hundred years, by the grace of a catchy Act of Settlement, the English throne was well occupied by a succession of portly archdukes of Hanover. The initial one, Georg Ludwig, known as George I (1660-1727), a grandson of James I, was forever in his carriage to Hanover and considered his royal obligation a drab task under a bad climate. He never bothered to acquire a knowledge of the English language, and communicated with his British ministers in rather poor school Latin. He left government pretty much to his ministers, especially Sir Robert Walpole. In a sense, his political alliances were well planned by professionals to secure his throne and his influence. Quite a few titles of British aristocracy, such as the Countess of Darlington, the Duchess of Kendal and others appointed by His Majesty, were mere German servant girls constituting part of his stable of mistresses. In the case of British, as well as Spanish, aristocracy, it is as well not to delve too deeply into the type of service rendered to the high court and rewarded by aristocratic privileges and titles.

The other of the indifferent Hanoverians was Augustus Peter, known as George II, King of Great Britain and Ireland 1727-1760. The dominant figure in his reign was William Pitt, protagonist of an incessant war policy. One could say that Pitt considered war and aggressive expansion to be the normal temper of political existence. George II, on his own and with Pitt's advice, so contrived matters that during his reign England never had a single year without war entanglement. The King himself was almost illiterate, had neither knowledge nor understanding of any of the arts or sciences. Still, some of his officials managed, in plaques and in documents, to attribute to him the creation of the German university of Göttingen and the British Museum.

His successor was Friedrich Wilhelm, commonly known as George III (b. 1738, d. 1820). He was a rather determined king, and changed his prime ministers with rapidity until he found in Lord North the kind of man who would be the king's gentleman. Baron North was directly responsible for some of the intolerable acts passed under George III as an infringement upon the freedom and dignity of the American people. His support in Parliament of the Townshend Acts was a major factor in their becoming law. The refusal of the American colonies to be taxed without representation brought about the attempt by British troops to enforce these overbearing laws, and led to the Boston Massacre and similar

106

incidents. The British policy of coercion and suppression can be directly attributed to Lord North, the most influential adviser of a poorly witted king who based his government to a considerable extent upon bribe and privilege. After the loss of the American colonies North resigned and gave way to William Pitt the Younger and others.

As the years went by, the King's mental deterioration became progressive. In 1810 he was declared permanently insane and the Prince of Wales assumed the Regency. For a man of limited mental capacity, George III was obsessed with an irrepressible desire for absolute rule. In his pathological fear of opposition he was responsible for the Aliens' Bill, and similar suppressive measures, including the abolition of the *habeas corpus* act. Like his predecessors, he was forever involved in aggressive military enterprises. In the fall of 1800 he managed to unite Ireland to England after a most savage attack against the Irish Catholic population.

In 1820 his son succeeded him officially. The Regent, Friedrich August, known as George IV (b. 1762, d. 1830), was perhaps the worst wastrel upon the English throne since Henry VIII. He was a reckless gambler, a squanderer of the country's funds, much of which he obtained in the most shameful manner, and given to seemingly irrepressible debauchery. He gave up his first marriage to the Catholic Maria Anne Fitzherbert for the sum of £682,000, which Parliament agreed to pay provided that he would make a political marriage with Princess Caroline of Brunswick. In view of his embarrassing private life, his governmental functions were severely curtailed by Parliament, and even the British Army refused to elevate him to a rank above colonel, fearful of how he might use increased military authority.

His public maltreatment of his second wife added to his considerable unpopularity. While he took little interest in the affairs of state, he somehow managed, for unknown considerations, to manipulate political appointments. Even after his succession to the throne from the Regency his decadent habits and his corrupt conduct didn't change. When he appeared in public on various occasions he was attacked by the people of London. As in the case of similar distasteful individuals who have worn a crown, he was protected by a certainly obsolete tradition, and by the pitiful dedication to such tradition of frequently outstanding men who upheld

107

this scoundrel as if he were a man of grace, because they respected the grace of the Crown more than they despised the ugliness of the wanton.

The amazing thing is that during the reign of the four horrible Hanoverians the English Crown extended its empire over all continents of the globe; by ruthless exploitation of its given resources and daring expeditions of conquest it enriched its treasury; it developed its war vessels to supreme power and its diplomacy of political interference in a manner unmatched by any other country of the time. Exploiting the weaknesses of the early discoverers, especially those of Spain, Portugal, France and Holland, the Crown managed by the use of its all-powerful fleet to rob the robbing conquistadors of their loot. In India and other Asiatic countries, as well as in the Americas, the British expeditionary forces succeeded in reducing, and often even completely annexing, the holdings of these colonialist powers.

And with every conquest their power grew and their riches increased, as they used the newly occupied territories, not as places of colonization or development, but rather as territories for ruthless exploitation.

It is true that later on these acts of selfishness came home to roost, but for generations one-fourth of the world lived in misery for the greater glory of a crown that more often than not rested on ill-chosen heads.

COLONIES AND COLOR LINE

If making amends could nullify nefarious acts, then the British have done much to erase from the memory of mankind the evils of their wanton imperialism, ruthless colonialism, and dastard slave trading in centuries so close to our memory that we can almost smell the stench of the misdemeanor.

While the Spanish, the Portuguese and, to a lesser degree, the French and the Dutch, set out, from the fifteenth century, on the seaward push for gold, gems and savage gain in blacks, the British, watching for a century or more the sea-faring appropriators, decided not to join the world-wide brigandry upon the colored people. They preferred to attack the pirates and take the loot from the ships upon the oceans
108

and from the safaris in the jungle, and the lands from the insecure conquerors.

Queen Elizabeth was the early mastermind of the grand international piracy which began the race on the Spanish Portuguese coasts, and ended with great battles against the French and Dutch on continents near and far.

One of the great steps toward the exploitation of the people of Asia was the formation of the East India Trading Company, created by the lusty Queen, and chartered by the amenable Parliament in the year 1600. Many books have been written about the sinister exploits of this trading monopoly, which for almost three hundred years sapped the strength, hopes, faith and virtue from the marrow of the people of India and China. Over the decades they systematically and relentlessly destroyed the village handicraft industries in Asia, lying prostrate at their mercy—of which they had as little as the cannons or bayonets they commanded. Indian cotton and jute were expropriated with only a pittance of formal compensation, and exported to England to be resold at a price thoroughly destructive to the native industries. This process of expropriation was easily encouraged by the undue taxation which was imposed upon the Asians as the price for British rule. Unable to meet these taxes, the once-prosperous peasants of India became deeply indebted tenants of the new landlord.

The city of Dacca, the textile center of early nineteenth-century India, for instance, lost 85 percent of its population between 1815 and 1837. Self-supporting communities all over the Indian subcontinent were reduced to dirt farming with the most primitive ancient implements in order to supply the new masters an easy surplus of agricultural products, and for themselves the means of bare existence. Small, independent agricultural and domestic industry almost entirely disappeared from the Indian scene, victims of English exploitative commerce from which until this very day the people of India have not recuperated.

The native handloom industry fell victim to Lancashire exports, which, with their low machine prices, reduced the Indian weavers to absolute wretchedness. By this process the starving and unemployed weavers were forced into beggarly tenant farming.

The prosperous communities of India, with their domestic
109

crafts and industries, became a thing of the past. With the elimination of this large middle class the peasants were compelled to sell their surplus products to the British at prices which had no relation to their worth. The progressive proletarianization of the townspeople and farmers continued, as did the decrease in the holdings of the average agriculturist. In a village in Poona the average holding dropped from forty acres in 1771 to seventeen acres in 1818. The peasants in India, as well as in British-controlled sections of China, fell prey to tax holders and money lenders and, by the first quarter of the nineteenth century, the typical picture of India's population was a million beggars to one prince. It may take a hundred years for the Indian community to walk the road back from ruination to its final independence and triumph.

While the British destroyed the village communities, they encouraged and preserved a subservient feudalism personified by corrupt and greedy princes and maharajas. Indeed, this type of double exploitation by the foreigner as well as the regal princeling even to this day has not yet been entirely eliminated. In 1857 the great mutiny occurred by native military forces, the Sepoys, employed by the British to secure their monarchistic policies. As was to be expected, poor leadership and lack of an over-all plan on the part of the frustrated garrisons, and the superior military equipment and means of communication held by the British foreboded the inevitable victory of the foreigners. The mutiny was suppressed, and vengeance was exacted upon the defeated in a manner that aroused the indignation of right-thinking people all over the world. Volunteer hanging parties of the British went from district to district executing the unarmed Indians on the slightest provocation or with no provocation at all. Around Allahabad alone eight thousand men, women and children were slaughtered.

However, the East India Company, held responsible for these atrocities, was finally dissolved. But the humiliation and exploitation · of the people of India continued until broken by the new awakening of the spirit of freedom after the Second World War.

The British rule over India against the will and on the back of its people was based on commercial greed and the lust for political power, which culminated in Queen Victoria's assumption of the title "Empress of India." Considering the wretched lot of the people of India, it should at least have been modified to "Empress over India." At no time did India represent more for the Crown than hunting grounds for commercial use and abuse. The natives had no rights and no privileges, no representation, and were given no dignity, no regard in matters of social status, no respect in religious ritual, and no opportunity to rise above the status of servitude in the penny pay of the foreign lords. A mere British boy of a lieutenant in the occupying forces of India could afford half a dozen servile Indians at his beck and call, so cheap were Indian hands. Only utter ignorance of conditions as they were could have permitted the bonneted queen to hang in her tearoom the gold-engraved diploma of the brazen self-assumption, "Empress of India."

Intimately linked with the activities of the East Indian Company in India were its excursions into China. One of its most odious enterprises was the intensification of opium horticulture in India, especially in Bengal, and since 1773 its importation into China under political pressure. In 1820 the Chinese government prohibited all traffic in opium, which led to the infamous Opium War with England. The cannons of Great Britain won again, and the British treasury was enriched immensely by this traffic, which has ever since degraded the people of China. The compulsory opium export into China by the East India Company is one of the ugliest pages in the rather depressing book of British history, and one that the people of Asia are not likely to forget.

One could perhaps say that some of the rulers the British expelled in their conquest of India, such as the king of Delhi, were weaklings, and that some of the ruling princes of old were selfish and gluttonous, like the Prince of Hyderabad. Be this as it may, the weakness of native governments does not excuse the atrocities of European colonizers.

By and large, the colonizers of the fifteenth, sixteenth and seventeenth centuries, referring to themselves as missionaries and discoverers, were no more than gold-and-gem-greedy pirates flying the cross at the bow and the black skull at the masthead. The colonizers of the eighteenth century and the early nineteenth century were slave hunters and territorial expansionists, and those of later decades were in the race for new markets, new mines and new plantations.

111

The colonizers of the nineteenth century in its second half divided Africa and Asia as gentlemen would a common hunting ground.

But the hunt is over and the colored nations of Africa and Asia have learned to live on their feet instead of on their knees.

With Nagaika and Sextant

Peter I (b. 1672 d. 1725)

Euphemistically referred to as "The Great," the Czar of Russia was named by his own edict Emperor. His despotic cruelty created early opposition, in whose rank was to be found his own son Alexis. Peter had the boy placed in a torture chamber in Moscow, where he finally expired his soul in 1718, chained on top of metal spikes. Peter's reign was given to chronic aggression in all four directions. With a newly organized army and navy, he conquered Karelia, Ingermanland, Livonia, segments of Poland, Baku, Astrakhan, Derbent and other territories, some of which, however, were liberated from him in later years.

Peter was perhaps the most classic example of a blue-blood megalomaniac who with equanimity considered all inhabitants under his power his personal subjects, and frequently treated the boyars and bishops not very differently from the serfs. He abolished the authority of the Church as constituted by the Patriarchate, and placed it under the Holy Synod, under the direction of a civil service Procurator appointed by himself. It was a type of Henry VIII reformation, which made him the undisputed master of all Church property. Following the example of the corpulent English monarch, he dismissed his wife and made a Livonian peasant girl of doubtful past the Empress. This woman, later known as Catherine I, had the distinction of living for some time as mistress of Peter's lieutenant, Menshikov, among others. In fact, Menshikov was persuaded to relinquish Catherine to his kingly master. The courts of Europe used to regale themselves with first-hand reports of the drunken orgies arranged for and by this alleged creator of modern Russia. Indeed, he died an early death during one of these excesses.

Peter's military ambitions caused him to make supreme efforts toward raising the technological level of Russia and

to improve the fiscal status of the state so thoroughly sub-
ordinated to his will. Like Stalin (who has often been com-
pared to him, and not without cause), he imported hundreds
of technicians and specialists from the West, many of whom
he hired personally on trips abroad. His next step was to
establish large factories financed by merchants whom he
made absolute masters in their domain. The workers in these
new factories of Czar Peter were designated serfs of the
employer and, like the peasants within the realm of the great
landowners, received no wages, only tokens. These serfs in
factories and pits, as well as on the great landed properties,
were tied to the bench or soil and owed their employers undisputed servility without any right of appeal or even protest.
The employers in the factories as well as the landowners had
the right to indict and try personally on the spot every serf,
male or female. These workers were surrendered in per-
petuity at the time of hiring.

It stands to reason that such compulsory labor would serve
to develop industry and agricultural production most favorably
to the sole profiteer of this process, namely the Emperor himself. This new autocracy of great landowners and industrialists was further strengthened by the edict of 1714, pro-
hibiting an owner to break up his estate as an heredity
measure.

From the miserable tokens the serfs received they had to
pay a poll tax to the Crown.

The overwhelming masses of Russia under Peter's predecessors, and more so yet under his successors, were serfs of
either the Czar's armed forces, or the Czar's landed proprie-
tors, or the Czar's industrialists.

To operate this extensive machinery of exploitation of labor
and direct taxation of all individuals, a separate class of civil
servants was created under a system of hierarchy by appoint-
ment of the Czar himself and under his personal control.

The new governors of each province, the clergy, the land
rich and the factory rich, the officers of the new navy and
the other extensive armed forces—all the multifarious opera-
tions of state and social life—were in the grip of one man,
serving the whim of one man—and a malevolent one at that.
How close a resemblance indeed to Stalin! In his irrepressible
modesty, the Czar moved the seat of government to the west,
in the newly conquered Baltic territories, naming it St. Petersburg—a play on the name perhaps, like the city of Constan-

tinople, or the city of Stalingrad, or the state of Virginia (the last one, for sure, only an ironic reference to the lusty Queen of England).

Peasant revolts against the outrages of Czarism, like the one led by Stenka Razin, occurred before and after Peter, but were unable however to withstand the gigantic military forces falling upon them. Peter even broke the power of the old nobility and that of the king-making military group, the Straltsi. On all men opposing him he practiced most sadistic vengeance; his cruelty toward those standing in his way was abominable. Here, too, we are reminded of Stalin's path to glory, littered with the heads of friends, opponents and disbelievers. Like Stalin, Peter enjoyed presenting those about to die (including his own son) in a mock trial before the public.

It has been said that Czar Peter sponsored research in the sciences, especially ballistics and geography, and that he increased literacy among his subjects. It is only reasonable that the man who planned war against the king of Sweden, the sultan of Turkey, and other neighbors would have need of greatly improving the state of the sciences in his rather backward country, since even in his day military success depended strongly upon scientific and industrial capacity. You cannot make artillery and operate it without a good knowledge of physics and mathematics, and for navigation meteorology and geography are essential, as the building of roads and vehicles for transportation is for land warfare. To operate successfully the extensive machinery of a feudal government one needs the services of many tens of thousands of literate persons, and for one's own social entertainment and grandeur —especially, for a man like Peter, who never lost the feeling of being a parvenu—one would ape the courts of the West with their music, poetry, dance and the theater, although the laurels of aesthetic sponsorship go not to this vicious epileptic, but rather to a later monarch, Catherine, called among many other names the least pertinent one, "the Great."

We find in the reign of Peter this almost typical promotion of learning at the direction of a self-seeking, aggressive and obnoxiously murderous ruler. In addition to various institutions of learning and state administration, Peter caused special schools to be opened, among them the Cannoneers' School in 1699, the Artillery and Navigation School in 1701, and the Marine Academy in 1715. Such learning is encouraged, or rather compelled, for the very same reason as military preparations are intensified and oppressive government is instituted. Learning is introduced for ulterior motives of aggression against a foreign neighbor, and suppression of the native citizenry. Science and technology, agriculture and schooling, road building and exploration, research and training—all are mere tools of imperialist purpose in such cases, under tyrannical government and in no way designed so that the people themselves may lead a better and fuller life.

The people in Russia under Peter were reduced to common serfdom and were slaves to the plough, the machine or the rifle. No thought was given to their happiness. They were just one great commune, a terrified community of desperately poor and desperately humiliated humanity, reduced to servitude at the behest and for the benefit of an ambitious and selfish Caesarian and his band of supporting landowners and merchants.

If during his reign and that of his successors Russia developed men and women of considerable distinction in science, literature and the arts, it was not because of Czarism, but rather in spite of it.

Peter's daughter Elizabeth (Petrovna), a latter-day successor to her father's throne by way of incarceration and finally strangulation of the rightful successor, young Ivan, was a connoisseur of art and science. She established the University of Petersburg as well as the Petersburg academy of art.

In ostentatious religiosity she encouraged church architecture and observance. She herself led a life of most flagrant debauchery at her court, dominated by intrigue and assassination. Her bed companions changed almost nightly. These affairs, however, were all too frequently accompanied by the gruesome and bloody elimination of rightful spouses and fiancées. One of her young lovers, the Ukrainian shepherd Rasumofski, was raised to marshal and had somewhat of a position as her morganatic husband. This secret union however in no way interfered with her nightly hunts for boy lovers. Elizabeth engaged in frequent wars of aggression and expansionistic maneuvers.

The Nymph of Petersburg

Catherine II (1729-1796). A German princess married to Czar Peter II ascended to the throne of all the Russians by having one of her many lovers, Orlow, assassinate her spouse on July 17, 1762, at the castle Ropscha. Among her many known, official courtiers during her marriage and after were Graf Serge Soltykow, the Polish Count Stanislaus Poniatowski, the said Gregor Orlow, the inimitable Gregor Potemkin, and a score of nameless officers and soldiers of the guard. Under considerably theatrical circumstances she had herself proclaimed "Mother of the Fatherland" by appointed representatives of all classes. She outdid Peter the Emperor in wars of occupation and aggression, as well as in diplomatic chicanery and blackmail. She conquered from the Turks the coastlands on the north of the Black Sea, drove the Khan of the Tartars from the Crimea, and participated in the cold-blooded dissection of Poland.

During all these bloody military affairs and political intrigues she managed to carry on an authentic intellectual correspondence with the great representatives of the era of enlightenment—Voltaire, Montesquieu, Diderot, Holbach and Grimm. Indeed, she considered herself an ardent devotee of enlightenment, at least as far as penning epistles was concerned. While at home she sharpened and broadened the subjugation of the serfs and, if such was possible, further deepened the antagonism between the common man and the gilded or landed employers.

To strengthen the economic position of the gentry, Catherine issued extensive grants of palace lands and serfs to the nobility upon whom her power rested. At the same time, the exploitation of state-owned serfs became more intense as the military adventures and the Paris-aping wasteful court expenses increased. The luxuries of the "Mother of the Fatherland," including innumerable invitations to foreign artists, paramours and specialists, as well as the rising costs of the upkeep of her gigantic armed forces, were all taken out of the hide of the peasants, the miners and the factory laborers. The poll tax already extorted by the Emperor Peter from every male member of the serfs' households was increased from two rubles a year to five rubles. Many of the so-called free workers could no longer feed their families, and the purchase and sale of serfs became a common practice. At the time of Catherine the Magnificent more than half of the population of Russia lived in servitude, subject to the cruel will of their employers. The working hours of the laborer and peasant, miner and common soldier, were from sunup to sundown, and never less than twelve hours a day. Nowhere in Europe was feudal oppression as flagrant and uninhibited as in the land of Catherine II, the great connoisseur of philosophical enlightenment. In 1764, only two years after the assassination of her husband Peter II, Catherine took over all church property from the monasteries, distributing the land and serfs among her aristocratic supporters as well as the state. The state of course meant no less than her own person, since the total treasury of Russia was at the disposal of her bejeweled hands, dealing it out on the advice and direction of her respective favorites. In that year alone over two million male and female serfs were converted into state-owned "economy peasants" (*ekonomichekiye krest-yani*).

In the same era the practice of selling serfs even without land was intensified. Some members of the nobility even managed to sell some of their serfs to the army as recruits.

This monstrous condition led to the great rebellion under the leadership of Yemelyan Ivanovich Pugachev in 1773. From the far steppes and from distant shacks and huts streamed thousands of peasants, Cossacks, Tartars and runaway serfs, forming a powerful revolutionary army. Pugachev proclaimed the abolition of serfdom and his troops quickly overran the lower Volga districts of the Ural region. However, the defeat of the ill-equipped troops was inevitable. Pugachev was captured and decapitated in Moscow. The widespread rebellion motivated the monarch of enlightenment to consider administrative reforms, namely, to increase the power and the privileges of the landowners and merchants over their serfs, and to solidify more firmly the miserable condition of servility in which the masses of the people lived.

Taking her cue from Emperor Peter, the lusty Czarina established widespread internal colonization in Russia. Thousands of foreign specialists in all fields of endeavor were invited, and even large settlements of western agriculturalists were encouraged. The now gigantic realm of Russia was

117

reorganized administratively, and schools opened in all larger cities to train civil servants, technicians, scientists, engineers, accountants and military specialists to meet the increasing demands of the state apparatus, so deftly handled by the Czarina. She herself was given to writing plays for the court stage in Petersburg and enchanting essays on liberal topics. It may be said that she even drew up a code of law, based on the writings of Montesquieu; however, this literary fragment never left her boudoir desk.

Catherine II was undoubtedly a highly educated person. Her life and deeds, however, prove conclusively that knowledge in itself is not a virtue, and talent alone not a blessing, unless they are guided by a feeling for humanity. Catherine II, in spite of her cultural background, lived and died a most vicious oppressor of a great nation, over which she made herself master by assassination. Her erudition made her not better, only more dangerous, and far from ameliorating her evil actions, made them all the more formidable and more effective.